THE FAMILY AS PATIENT

THE FAMILY AS PATIENT

*The Origin, Nature,
and Treatment of Marital
and Family Conflicts*

HORST E. RICHTER

*Translated from the German
by Denver and Helen Lindley*

A CONDOR BOOK
SOUVENIR PRESS (EDUCATIONAL &
ACADEMIC) LTD

My thanks are due to all my colleagues who since the founding of the psychosomatic clinic at the University of Giessen in 1962 have labored with me to advance psychoanalysis and its social applications. Their critical suggestions have played a decisive part in the creation of this book.

Horst E. Richter

Giessen
March 1970

CONTENTS

THE FAMILY AS PATIENT

FOREWORD

From a preliminary conversation with a couple who have come to introduce their daughter as a patient

Mother, referring to the daughter: The girl has lost contact with everyone. She shuts herself off completely. She barely speaks to me. I can no longer get to her. When I tell her this, she gets furious at me. She's in a dreadful state.

Mother, a half hour later: I'm really crazy about my daughter. We could do so much together . . . My husband is so wrapped up in his work . . .

Father, interrupting her: Well yes, but you certainly can't say I'm not home enough . . .

Mother: Even so, most of the time you're preoccupied with your own affairs. I don't blame you for that. But actually I often feel that I'm alone.

Doctor: You came here asking me to treat your daughter for loss of contact. However, I can see now that all of you feel excessive demands are being made on you by the others. You (*to the mother*) suffer from a lack of companionship. Your daughter and your husband are obviously reacting as though they were expected to give more of themselves than they are able to. It's a case of not understanding one another.

Mother: You're absolutely right. I for one can't stand it any longer. I think I need treatment every bit as much as my daughter does.

1

Psychotherapy and Social Reality

A new and highly useful branch of psychoanalysis is the investigation and treatment of group conflicts. Many psychoanalysts no longer regard the individual only as the owner of a psychic apparatus which may require diagnosis and therapy. Instead, they have learned to relate the psychological condition of a person to the make-up of the group he is part of, usually his family. In particular they focus much more on the effect of conscious and, even more important, unconscious interchanges within the family in determining which individual will suffer a psychic disturbance, what form the disturbance will take, and the course it will follow.

Often a psychically ill person cannot recover as long as his family life is seriously upset. A family, for instance, may use a chronically unsuccessful member or a seemingly hopeless problem child as a scapegoat to drain away its collective tension, which would otherwise be unbearable. His psychical disturbance springs from the special role unconsciously forced upon him by his family, and psychotherapeutic treatment may fail because the family will refuse to release its scapegoat. But even if psychotherapy succeeds in freeing this victim from the role thrust upon him, there is a danger that the family may then find another, no less disastrous way of channeling its collective tension. Thus, if a child stops being the safety valve for his parents' marital troubles, then the parents, to compensate, may pick on another of their children. Or, in similar circumstances, a family whose weakest member refuses to be victimized by the conflict may then cope with its inner tension by turning against the outside world in hatred and disgust. The family's unresolved conflict will remain concealed as long as it succeeds in remaining united against an outside enemy, being always, irrationally, on the attack. This kind of situation occurs, for example, in families where one member, released from a neurotic masochism, is no longer willing to be the target for the family's unresolved aggression.

We see from such cases that the closer an individual's disturbance is connected with overriding group conflicts, the greater the danger that purely individual therapy will not work. Or, if the therapy is effective, the group will simply select someone else to burden with its problems.

This book will consider the meaning of these group relationships in the light of the increasing importance of family-oriented therapy and its effect on marriage and family counseling. Remarkable progress has been made in applying psychoanalytical knowledge to interpersonal conflicts. Psychological counseling work with married couples and with parents and children is being done on an improved scientific level, shedding more and more the dilettante pragmatism which hampered it for so long.

But these improvements in the application of psychoanalysis —from individual to family conflicts, from the treatment of a single patient to family therapy—raise a question of basic importance. If it is true that injury to an individual results often from overriding group conflicts in the family, isn't it also true that family problems often stem from prevalent social conditions? And, in that case, is it enough to treat psychotherapeutically the tension within a family if at least part of the reason for it may lie in social factors outside the family?

Finally, pursuing such considerations to the end, one comes

across the objections of the new radical left to any form of psychotherapy whatever. The radical-left factions argue that our repressive social system is harmful to families as well as individuals to such a degree that it is not private psychotherapy but only a revolutionary change of the entire social system that makes any sense. And they accuse psychotherapy of upholding the system by helping the problem-riddled individual or family to adapt to it. Absurdly enough, psychic health today means that one feels well in this unhealthy social order and functions well for its purposes. According to this view, psychoanalysts and psychotherapists are conformists supporting the system. They misuse their psychological insight to reduce discomforts and conflicts, or they and their patients avert their eyes from the destructive social forces and try to ignore the fact of constant and powerful repression in the individual's private life.

This objection is a serious one and calls for analysis to be extended beyond family conflicts to the causes of conflict in the encompassing social institutions, and finally to the general structure of our social order. For just as an individual neurosis can often be understood as the symptom of a family conflict, so a family neurosis can often be interpreted as the symptom of something wrong in society. Health cannot be defined as adapting harmoniously to a harmful social situation, and it is certainly not a valid ideal for the psychotherapist.

Some unjustified assumptions, however, underlie the arguments of radical critics of psychotherapy. At the top of the list is the theory, untenable in such an oversimplified form, that all neuroses are merely by-products of the social system, that if the system were to be revolutionized there would be no more neuroses and consequently no further need for psychotherapists. We will discuss this illusion later in detail, but the point should be made now that almost all psychoanalysts believe that our present form of society is in many respects inadequate and is in need of change. Many of the new leading social critics not only make use of the methods and insights of psychoanalysis, but some of them are practicing psychoanalysts themselves. Their concern over the society's need for creative changes leads many analysts to undertake, in addition to their professional duties, work as investigators and publicists on social problems. In fact, the psychoanalytical cast of mind leads one to study sociocultural problems in which irrational methods of suppression and other ways of concealing conflicts need to be brought to light and eliminated. Psychoanalysts attempt to analyze these collective neurotic phenomena on the basis of the inescapable analogy with individual clinical cases. In this effort, of course, they must depend heavily on the cooperation of trained empirical social investigators if they hope to produce truly reliable findings in the field of political sociology.

The demand, however, that psychoanalysis should be used entirely in such social analysis and no longer in the clinical field is hard to understand. What would become then, for example, of people who, as a result of the inadequacies of education, suffer from neurotic illnesses? Are they to be cynically comforted with the thought that, after the recommended improvements in the educational system have been implemented, a later generation will have less to suffer? Haven't they a right to psychiatric treatment for their acquired disabilities? And what would become of others who, under sociocultural pressures, develop psychogenic disturbances from which the psychotherapist cannot completely shield them? Take the example of a child whose parents, conforming to the society's exaggerated ideals of accomplishment, impose an education based purely on ambition and make him neurotic? The psychotherapist surely should attempt to make the parents and teachers more understanding, and perhaps through psychotherapy give the child some protection against harmful outside pressures. It would be inhuman to refuse this personal help on the grounds that society must first revise its notions of accomplishment.

The psychoanalyst may conclude that the demand for his voluntary withdrawal in the interests of a purely political activism shows the same kind of inhumanity this activism is supposed to abolish. How can the healing of psychically ill individuals or families be seriously considered a reprehensible digression? There is, however, some reason to suspect that certain extreme groups may be counting on the unchecked spread of psychic suffering to help to achieve their aims.

But this sort of inhuman strategy is based on illusion. Those suffering from neurotic ailments are the least competent of all to cure society. Only people who are able to deal with their own problems in some measure openly, and in any case without serious neurotic inhibitions, can effect a change of social norms in the direction of tolerance and freedom from repression. The neurotic, as Freud[35]* has shown, must continually reproduce his unresolved conflicts, as a result of an unconscious repetition compulsion. However passionately he may agitate for progressive social goals, he will never be able to help to establish any kind of liberty that he does not accept within himself. At the moment of victory over external oppressors, to his own horror and that of his allies, he will be forced through a neurotic compulsion to throw away the opportunities he has fought for. This is one reason why work on family neuroses and individual neuroses is far more important than its critics of the radical left suggest. Successful psychotherapy gives the family or the individual the possibility of dealing with personal problems more courageously and openly, of understanding them more clearly, and reducing the destructive, irrational effects they may have. In this way, successful psychotherapy makes a contribution to the establishment of freer forms of education and human association in general.

Many critics of psychotherapy respond imperturbably: The high-minded objectives you therapists proclaim for your treatment have no reality at all in what you actually do. You announce, of course, that you try in every case for a broadening of consciousness and a strengthening of the sense of social responsibility; that you help people to go about their social duties freed from repression and authoritarian lines of defense. But this is all in fact an illusory promise, for what you actually practice contradicts these admirable principles. In reality, you simply help your clients to a better private defense against damaging social relationships or even, by denying that any conflict exists, to an identification with disastrous social structures.

When challenged in this way, psychoanalysis should first

* The superior numbers are references to the bibliography at the end of the book.

apply its techniques for unmasking self-delusion to itself. We know that methods for increasing repression or enforcing conformity in a repressive society are contrary to the principles of psychoanalysis, but, nevertheless, we should consider whether these methods are in fact sometimes supported under the guise of psychoanalysis or psychotherapy. Our critics' accusations can be summed up in two general points, which will be answered in detail:

1. Analytical psychotherapy removes the patient too far from reality, by dealing exclusively with inner psychic conflicts and their treatment.

2. The medical goal, freedom from suffering, frequently misleads analytical psychotherapy into an unconcerned "adjustment therapy."

Point 1

The first accusation is based on two facts which can be interpreted and evaluated very differently.

Psychoanalysis and all the procedures of psychotherapy derived from it (for example, analytical family therapy or group therapy) are principally based on the use of introspection. Patients observe their inner reactions and reflect on the motives for their behavior. In family and group therapy, the background processes among the persons involved are also studied and treated. The subject matter of the therapy in all cases is feelings, wishes, defense mechanisms, which are uncovered through introspection. The outer world is taken into account to the extent that, during the treatment, the question is raised as to how the patients behave toward external reality—and why. The reverse of this question—what does the outer world do to the patients?—plays only a very minor role in individual therapy. In family therapy, however, it is taken into consideration insofar, for example, as the parents of a sick child are seen as agents of society.

And so it must be admitted that in general the technique of introspection now in use aims precisely at giving a patient, for the time being, a longer perspective on his relations with the outside world. In this sense, the judgment is entirely correct that psychoanalysis removes people from social reality. But the goal of this technique is quite different from what the critics assume: not a permanent lessening of this relationship, but only its clarification.

Psychically disturbed individuals only partially experience social reality as it actually is. They deal with a caricature of reality intermingled with many unconscious projections of their own inner problems. The long introspective process toward self-knowledge in analytical therapy teaches patients first of all how much of reality they formerly saw distorted by their unconscious conflicts, or did not see at all. The length and thoroughness of this process, if properly conducted, reveal to many patients for the first time a picture of their personal situation and also the general social situation, cleansed of neurotic distortions. They can then devote themselves with unhampered energies to their social tasks, which are now properly understood. In a model analytical treatment there is no conflict between introspective self-knowledge and meaningful social involvement; on the contrary, the relationship is one of mutual support.

To achieve the goal of analytical treatment, analysts have to adapt their methods to the ever changing requirements of therapy. When analytical treatment in general was substantially shorter, an analysis might be conducted as though in a cloister, with the patient for the comparatively brief duration requested to withdraw into himself and the analysis, and to refrain as far as possible from making important practical decisions. This ideal had to be abandoned when treatments were lengthened in the interest of greater thoroughness, and it became obvious that the patient could not postpone practical decisions for so long. The approach to analysis had to change substantially—so much so that the practical activity of the patient during analysis is no longer considered basically an "agitation" disturbing to the analysis but rather an important aspect for analytical work. The continuous analysis and especially the strengthening of the patient's ego in its decision-making function have been repeatedly called for by Rangell, the president of the International

Psychoanalytical Association. He rightly expects an intensive investigation of the decision-making function to come up with theoretical insights of far-reaching importance: "To gain an understanding of the decision-making faculty in terms of depth psychology is perhaps the most urgent sociopsychological task that confronts us."

The critics of psychoanalysis are therefore wrong when they assume that psychoanalytical treatment—which for the most part they know only in its earlier stages—neglects the social relationships of patients and overemphasizes the inner psychic world.

Yet, in another respect, there is legitimate cause for concern. One hears now and then of psychotherapists who disregard all recent advances in psychoanalysis and are still reluctant to deal with their patients' activities in the outside world; they justify this position by regarding their patients' activities as really only evasions of or escape reactions to the therapeutic situation. As a result, the patients get the impression that the therapist wants to hear as little as possible about their day-to-day lives. This in fact introduces an authoritarian, moralizing element into the treatment, though it cannot be assumed that the patient and the therapist are aware of it.

On the contrary, it may be that both doctor and patient lean toward an "overidealization of the analysis" (Greenacre[42]). This kind of distortion of the therapeutic situation arises more readily in individual treatment than in group therapy, and it causes the analysis to become a kind of religious rite. Patient and analyst mutually support each other in the notion that psychoanalysis is enormously important, that it can accomplish anything. This overvaluation of the analysis stems from unresolved narcissistic needs and can turn the hours of mutual brooding and meditation into a marvelous oasis in the midst of an unsatisfactory or, worse still, frightening reality. In other words, the overvaluation of the analysis suggests a refuge: both patient and doctor keep their aggressive feelings out of the analytical situation by using them to deprecate the world outside (Greenacre[42]). Out of shared resentment, they interpret dangerous, unsympathetic social reality as having no importance whatever. With contempt

verging on actual disgust—product of their developing resentment—they downgrade reality and glorify with worshipful
devotion the psychic inner kingdom with its marvelous symbols
and mysterious dynamic processes. Here lies the real world, so
they firmly believe; the outside world is hardly more than appearance. And so they delude themselves into justifying their retreat from the demands of practical reality. Thus they have
devised a protective shield like those that idealistic metaphysical
systems once provided for their creators and adherents.

Such aberrant "treatment" does not deserve the name of psychoanalysis. When a therapist systematically encourages a patient in the fantasy that analysis has the power to sweep away,
like so many phantoms, all the problems of his relations with
outer reality, he is deceiving him. He is maneuvering him into
a narcissistic idealistic illusion and betraying his professional
undertaking to help him deal with the hidden problems of his
life. Instead, he is conducting a psychotherapy of "concealment."
Essentially this is a phobia shared, though disavowed, by
therapist and patient. The treatment, which should be a series of
tests and experiments in acquiring a freer attitude toward oneself and the world, is transformed into a protective refuge.
Finally, as this refuge becomes even more overidealized, presumably nothing further remains for the patient but to join those
pathetic individuals who, like addicts, for decades follow one
"analysis" with another because they cannot free themselves
from the illusion that only in analysis itself can they find life's
greatest fulfillment.

This is one way, then, in which the insights and techniques
of psychoanalysis can sometimes be dangerously misused. The
well-justified criticism of such practices, however, is aimed not
at psychoanalysis itself but at what is, literally, a betrayal of it.

Point 2

Current criticism of psychotherapy from the radical left is not
directed principally at this phobic, resentful overidealization of
analysis as explained above, but instead at an alleged psychotherapy of conformity. This sort of psychotherapy makes no

attempt to reduce the pressure of unresolved social problems created through ideological reaction formation and concealment, but simply to improve adaptation. Social reality in this case is not idealistically devalued but is accepted uncritically as an overpowering actuality; the patient must learn always to sacrifice his personal needs to accepted standards whenever there is a conflict.

This concept of the function of psychotherapy, whether avowed or not, has been influential for a long time, and even today it must be dealt with seriously.

Its persuasive power can be understood from the historic attempt to model psychological medicine on organic medicine. The M.D. works with a comparatively uncomplicated concept of the surrounding world: the organism finds itself in a relatively constant environment in which air pressure and temperature, composition of air and water, means of nourishment, micro-organisms, and other requisite elements make life and health possible. With a change to other surroundings, say to another climatic zone or to a different altitude, the organism must learn to adapt itself to its new milieu, perhaps by growing accustomed to a different kind of nourishment, by a change in metabolism, by an increase in red blood corpuscles to make up for reduced oxygen at greater altitudes, etc. Thus, maximum adaptability in the organism becomes the medical ideal. For a long time, an attempt was made in psychological medicine to work with a similar concept of the surrounding world. The system of accepted social standards was interpreted in somewhat the same way as the biological surroundings. Thus, the ideal individual would be the one best able to fit himself into extremes of differing social requirements without loss of well-being and functional efficiency.

Thought through to its logical conclusion, this results in the ideal of a man who, as a soldier in wartime, can shoot and kill and at the same time sleep as well, have as good an appetite, and be as free from anxiety as he would in peacetime after spending his day at his job. He remains "psychically normal" no matter how human or inhuman the social circumstances around him. The ambiguity of this uncritical concept of a psychosomatic ideal norm is unmistakable, for it is just those men who concern themselves about progress in humanizing social conditions who suffer most from inhuman conditions. If a sensitive, discriminating person, caught in a situation of massive injustice and brutality, develops sleeplessness, headaches, and the inability to work, these can be meaningful psychosomatic symptoms of a feeling that the situation is intolerable, appropriate alarm signals that the limits within which a differentiated personality can maintain his psychosomatic balance have been exceeded. From this point of view, the limitation of psychosomatic adaptability is seen as an altogether useful regulator; a narrow-minded medicine based on symptomology has for a long time effectively refused to recognize this fact.

It is a highly questionable practice automatically to classify psychic "adaptation disturbances" as medical defects or to treat them psychiatrically as reactivated childhood conflicts, without finding out whether a symptomless adaptation to the given social situation would not really be more disturbing than an unsuccessful one.

There are abundant examples of the bad light psychotherapy puts itself in when it mistakenly adopts the role of aiding a patient to conform at any price. Looking through the older psychiatric literature about so-called war neuroses, one rarely comes across the thought that the unprotesting adaptation of soldiers to a world of killing need not be the unqualified goal of psychotherapeutic intervention. In his psychiatric best seller, *Their Mothers' Sons,* E. A. Strecker even argues explicitly for a change in the American system of education (avoidance of maternal coddling), pointing to what he considers the shameful fact that in World War II many young Americans were or became unfit for military duty due to psychological disturbances.

The doubtful nature of an uncritical psychotherapy of adaptation need not necessarily be illustrated by such extreme situations as war. In everyday psychotherapeutic practice the doctor constantly has trouble deciding whether a given failure in psychological adaptation should be regarded as the individual's fault or, instead, as an alarm signal that he is being exposed to overwhelming social pressures. One must often recognize that symptoms, which in the usual medical sense indicate neurotic illness, are to be understood from a sociopsychological point of view as positive signs of a "healthy" resistance to a disastrous social situation. In such cases, an analytical psychotherapist fails in his duty if he regards himself simply as the healer of the neurotic symptoms or the repairer, as the case may be, of the particular psychic mechanism that produced those symptoms. Thereby, consciously or not, he would be identifying himself with a demand for conformity which in this social situation could not be justified. The psychotherapeutic "cure" of an individual in the sense that he finally learns to adapt unresistingly or without symptom formation to a damaging social role that has been forced upon him is in sharpest contradiction to the principles of psychoanalysis.

Now of course a psychotherapist from time to time may feel unable to make any change in a bad situation which his patient cannot cope with, and sometimes he has to recognize that he cannot help his patient to improve his crushing external relationships. But however unalterable the situation may seem, there is always the opportunity of supporting the patient so that he can at least consolidate whatever inner independence and freedom he has and gather strength for a later chance to modify the damaging outer situation, while in the meantime reducing his nagging self-torment.

Sometimes, however, psychotherapists have an opportunity, in cooperation with their patients, to alter the external factors producing the illness. Here a retreat to a simple "therapy of adaptation" would be completely inexcusable. Two examples illustrate this kind of opportunity.

A mother brings her ten-year-old daughter to a psychotherapist because the girl complains of lack of appetite at mealtimes and eats very little, and yet between meals constantly raids the refrigerator. The girl's trouble is easily enough classified in traditional fashion as "neurotic loss of appetite" combined with "compulsive eating." The mother plans to turn the child over to the therapist as a "patient" or, to be more exact, as a "miscreant," and to welcome her back once the defect has been corrected by treatment. The mother is acting simply as a client, as the healthy relative who brings the child for necessary treatment as though for an operation on her tonsils or appendix. It cannot be denied that many educational counselors have often blindly accepted the role offered them by mothers of this kind. They assume that the child's disturbed eating habits are to be viewed as an entirely individual behavioral difficulty which should be treated therapeutically. In alliance with the mother, they attempt to teach the child to "eat properly."

In reality, this ten-year-old girl's refusal to eat is a protest against a mother who is a tyrant, who severely limits the girl's freedom of activity and supervises everything she does. She also expects the child to express gratitude for everything that is "done for her," and the girl cannot assert herself against this tyranny. For the mother, eating plays a special role; it is one of her favorite instruments of control. The family must enjoy and praise her cooking; otherwise, she is instantly offended and shouts frightening moral reproaches. The father, who is just as incapable of standing up to his wife as the daughter is, frequently avoids family meals under the pretext of business duties. The daughter feels her father's secret opposition and knows that they are allies. Her alternation between not eating and secret gorging is principally a masked protest against her mother's domination, which has become unbearable. It is a nonverbal opposition at a point where the mother is especially vulnerable: the girl is punishing the mother for oppression by refusing food, something the mother cannot abide. Therefore, one can understand the girl's eating problem properly only if one sees it in connection with the mother's attitude. The disturbance is not in the child herself; rather, it is the communication in the family that is disturbed, primarily because of the unbridled and inconsiderate behavior of the mother. The girl's symptoms are signs of a desperate defense against a superior force, which in her helplessness and fear she has found no better way to cope with.

The daughter would perhaps have a chance of ridding herself of her symptoms if she were to learn to subjugate herself completely to her mother. Or perhaps she could find a less provocative form of resistance and thus in a less dangerous way protect herself against her mother, in much the same

fashion as the father does. Both these would be merely pallia-
tives. The therapist should attempt to appeal directly to the
mother and to bring her, through patient and probably very
difficult efforts, to give up her oppressive influence on the rest
of the family. The father, too, should be persuaded to stop
evading the issue through flight and bring the family problem
into open discussion. If the analyst avoids this therapeutic effort
with the whole family, he must eventually appear corrupt and
cowardly to the daughter, allowing himself to be manipulated
by her mother just as her father does, despite his supposed
expertise. And he would make it more difficult than ever for
the girl to overcome her dependency conflict.

Another example: Parents are always bringing children to
psychotherapists to have their offsprings' school work improve.
More often than not, however, scholastic troubles are the expression of conflicts that originally have nothing whatever to
do with the work. By a bad performance at school, for instance,
a child takes revenge on parents who refuse him most of his
wishes but want to compensate for their own unsatisfied ambitions through their child's success at school. The child's
"laziness" is his last chance to break away from an enforced
role and preserve a remnant of freedom. Actually, his "poor
performance" represents the remains of his psychological health.
Here the child is still acting as himself; he has not yet been
absorbed into the role which his ambitious, egocentric parents
wish to thrust upon him. Nevertheless, there are psychotherapists who take a child's unsatisfactory performance as a fault
automatically requiring therapy, just as a mechanic regards a
defect in a machine, without asking whether perhaps the child's
unwillingness to study might not indicate that the source of
the trouble is to be looked for in an entirely different direction
—to wit, in his parents.

This does not mean that when a child is failing in school
as a form of unconscious protest, the therapist should encourage him in his unwillingness to work. This form of protest,
in the long run, generally does more harm to the child than
to those he is trying to oppose. However, the child will presumably redevelop a spontaneous interest in doing well—though

perhaps not exactly in the areas preferred by his parents—as soon as he can feel that achievement is the result of his own free initiative and no longer a duty pressed upon him for the fulfillment of his parents' egoism. Therefore, the principal point of attack in treatment must first of all be the parents, who have to be made to see how their demands are proving traumatic to the child. Then one may discover that the parents believe they can endure their own painful awareness of inferior accomplishment only through absolute conformity to the particular ideals admired in their circle. Perhaps the psychotherapist can reduce their anxiety about this. Possibly, as so often happens, their ambition serves only as a compensation for feelings of self-doubt and guilt in some other area. If one can help allay these fears, the parents can perhaps modify the rigorous ideals of accomplishment they have imposed on the child. The very real pressure of social demands for accomplishment affects parents as well as children in our culture, and fixes limits to the effectiveness of the work of the psychotherapist, as already discussed.

To sum up, it can be granted to the critics of modern psychotherapy that they are right in warning against two excrescences of psychotherapy: first, the flight from unresolved social conflicts into an egocentric, introverted idealism which, out of resentment of social reality, is overvalued through ideological reaction formation; second, a more or less corrupt conformist therapy which, like that of reality denial, offends the very principles on which psychoanalysis is based. It is difficult, however, to prevent the misuse of the highly explosive insights and instrumental procedures of psychoanalysis by numerous phobic escapists and a few uncritical conformist psychotherapists. Yet one should be constantly alert to dangers of this sort. Badly handled psychotherapy can be no less damaging than undistorted psychoanalysis can be beneficial and liberating.

Modern criticism of psychotherapy, then, deserves credit for having helped to stimulate a self-critical attitude toward its possible misuses. On the other hand, more needs to be said about the hypercritical sociological polemics against psychotherapy.

The contention that neurotic sufferings arise simply from

sociocultural inequities is incorrect. The sociocultural factor is only one of the conditions favoring neuroses and psychosomatic illnesses. Hereditary psychology has established that various forms of neuroses and psychoses appear with a high degree of correspondence in identical twins, even when they have been separated immediately after birth and raised in entirely different environments. Thus, the hereditary factor has been under-estimated.

The extreme critics also neglect, in addition to the unalter-able biological factors, the influence of freedom in making personal decisions. As a psychoanalyst, one often sees neuroses that have arisen to a large extent from the overwhelming pressures of the outside world, but there are many others that are to a substantial degree the result of wrong choices that were not only wrong but could have been avoided. Individuals or families may shy away, by choice, from mastering problems they encounter. These problems, ignored out of fear, create increasing tensions, which finally result in neurotic symptom formations. And yet it has been proven that it is within the power of such people to deal with these pathogenic problems; often they need only a single sustained push through clarifying psychotherapeutic insight to solve actively and by themselves the problems that had previously made them lose heart.

In any case, the practical results of psychoanalysis con-tradict the impression given by defeatist sociological determinism that the individual or family is the helpless plaything of social forces. Despite harmful sociocultural pressures and the limit-ing effect of constitutional heredity, people do have a chance to work at their individual and group problems and uncover and eliminate the conflict-concealing mechanisms that cause the problems in the first place. Here psychoanalysis can provide the individual as well as the family with vital help. This work with small groups cannot, of course, replace the political struggle for a freer social system. But it is by no means rendered super-fluous by that struggle, to which in the long run it will make an effective contribution in the form of better-adjusted individuals.

People who throw away the chance to deal positively with their neurotic problems, in the hope that a revolutionary transformation of society will do it for them, are in reality giving evidence of a deep, depressive hopelessness.

The enmity toward psychotherapy of many radical groups reflects a kind of irrational resignation. Many deny that they share responsibility for their unresolved conflicts, because, out of depressive cowardice, they lack the courage to admit their personal shortcomings and come to terms with them. The picture of a world completely debased, with themselves as crippled victims, frees them from the feeling of personal responsibility for failure and is at the same time a huge, projected reflection of their own inner discouragement.

2

Family Problems in a Changing Society

The family is a stage on which the emotional forces of depression, fear, defensive stubbornness, and protest make dramatic appearances as the generations meet and clash. Frequently, too, one openly expressed depression collides with another that is disguised by repression and projection. In recent times particularly, families with growing children, high-school or college students, have often been shocked by the tensions that can quite unexpectedly reveal abysses between people who never previously doubted their harmonious solidarity. In a psychosomatic clinic, one sees in quick succession bewildered parents whose formerly well-adjusted children want to leave home, give up their studies, live in a commune, or simply roam about with their contemporaries. And many of these parents have prided themselves on the liberal way in which they raised these children: "There is absolutely no good reason for that youngster to throw everything away and run off!"

It is often not the young people who have suffered especially from authoritarian oppression who suddenly want to leave home. A great many cherished children from relatively liberal households are acting exactly the same way. Something compels them to seek their identities away from home, at times because they do not wish to accept as their own the protective, supportive, instructive representatives of their parents' world. The very attractiveness of an unusually idyllic parental home can strengthen the inner compulsion of a child to tear himself loose and with the help of an anti-establishment group of contemporaries seek out his own path. Of course, it is not always easy to separate in these cases what is neurosis, or simply fad, the suggestive suction of collective tendencies, from what is the compelling judgment of critical young people who believe they can no longer advance toward a new life style of their own except in this way.

This sort of stormy, divisive conflict with young people is almost the rule today, and it shows the new possibilities as well as the limits of family-oriented psychotherapy. *Possibilities,* because here is a problem whose solution concerns not only the new generation but the whole family and which can often be better treated in collective family sessions with a psychotherapist than in any kind of traditional individual therapy. *Limits,* because from time to time psychopathological and medicinal therapeutic insights are not adequate to exhaust the meaning of such phenomena and to provide categories for their treatment. Problems beyond the family intrude here, and to understand and solve them the techniques of the psychotherapeutic physician are not enough. It is therefore all the more important for the new generation of psychotherapists to apply themselves to a greater extent to sociology so as to better understand the interaction of the individual and the family with related social factors, and to make a better estimate of the therapeutic possibilities.

Today, in general, what is a psychically healthy family like? The very question assumes a change in standards of value. Nowadays certain internal tensions between parents, as well as between parents and children, are not only "no more than normal"; they are even sometimes important signs of intellectual vitality, positive indications of health in the family. The classical concept of harmony or lack of it has had to be revised. The presence of severe or even explosive conflicts is not what indicates a break in the family; it is the inability of the members to deal with tensions of this sort and to clear them up without mutual rejection or punishment and without driving some member into a state of symptom formation.

If we examine the various criteria of psychic health, we inevitably encounter the theoretical difficulties of defining psychic health and normality in general, a problem now being studied with varying degrees of success.* Obviously, the concept of what in psychological medicine is meant by "healthy" and "normal" is in a state of flux at the present time. If a subterranean, depressive mood, a kind of malaise, is sometimes characteristic of especially sensitive circles, then families who show signs of a similar malaise cannot be logically classified as abnormal. Clearly, we must recognize that in times of severe social tension there appear striking emotional reactions and attitudes that it would be unfair to label automatically as psychopathological phenomena requiring treatment. Discouragement, irritability, and, recently in the young, widespread moods of helplessness and attitudes of almost paranoid resentment are more—or, if one wants to turn it around, less—than disturbances requiring treatment. "More," in that they are caused by overriding sociological conditions; "less," in the sense that those involved are generally only slightly damaged, if at all. Psychological medicine must therefore extend the range of variation for what is normal: much that looks like illness from a symptomatic point of view is nevertheless not illness in the sense of traditional individual pathology. Symptoms that can be understood primarily as the signs of a critical phase in society do demand therapy, but the kind of therapy that comes to grips with the social conflicts.

One of the family problems that a psychotherapist considers specific to our times and in part unavoidable is constant discussions of and disagreement about sex.

The rejection of accepted standards of sexual behavior in public is reflected in the confusion of many families. The flood of sexual revelations in the various mass media, which shows

* Bibliography in D. Offer and M. Sabshin's *Normality* (New York, London, 1966).

a breakdown in the rigid standards of behavior, results in feelings of uncertainty and a loss of orientation. Some families even practice an inverted sexual moralism; instead of a freer, more tolerant attitude toward sexuality, they engage with missionary zeal in a paradoxical, often hygienically justified sex cult. Sex becomes a new goal of education. It is studied and progressively trained for in a manner that reminds one of the calisthenics and hygiene classes of athletes. Through nudist practices, compulsory sexual table-talk with children, etc., these people are proving to themselves their own courage and modernity—they easily forget that such exhibitionistic and voyeuristic performances are no more than the illusion of a real solution to the problem of sexuality and the anxieties connected with it. "Sex holds no mysteries for our children." Such is the boast heard from hysterical parents about their systematic efforts to educate their children in uncomplicated, "natural sex," thereby usually achieving only a rationalized overcompensation of their own repressed sexual anxieties—and those of their children. This at least is certain: the image of fearless sexual enthusiasm that our society exhibits today could convince only the superficial observer that a definitive working out of the problems of sexuality has really begun. It is nothing more than a transformation of the traditional defense against sex into a no less anxiety-ridden pseudo-hypersexuality. Intellectualizing the phenomenon makes it easier to separate—as well as to obscure—emotional problems whose mature solution, but not their illusory elimination, holds out genuine hope.

This more or less hysterical pseudo-hypersexuality, however, is found in only a small number of families, despite the temporary excitement they have aroused. Unpublicized, the classical defense tactic of conservative parents still prevails. This parental type is encountered much more often than any other in psychotherapeutic practice. These are the parents who mistakenly fear that a growing generation freed from imposed repressions and concealments would conjure up a chaotic state of general promiscuity. The classical psychoanalytical answers to these fears still hold good: such parents project upon and attribute to the young the dangers that, because of unresolved sexual conflicts within themselves, they have not been able to find any better protection for than through reaction formations. Also, sexual envy of the more vital young adds to the unconscious motives for asserting that youthful sexuality freed of taboos would badly distort our culture.

But if we are slowly learning that young people must find their own way to deal with their sexuality, then it follows that in the family, in school, by precept, etc., they should be allowed responsibility early so that they can gain practice in handling these problems. One can hardly expect "half children" to behave responsibly on their own in regard to their sexuality if they are not treated the same way in everything else. There are grotesque conceptions of developmental psychology bruited about regarding the confusion, blind impulsiveness, and unreasonableness supposedly typical of the age of puberty. This confused state is considered an unalterable biological burden, and it is vehemently denied that society, following ancient tradition, does all it can to delay the social maturing of the young, in direct opposition to biological acceleration. This is the pretext for the educational manipulations that are supposed to satisfy the requirements of children and young people during puberty.

It is undeniable that there are serious reasons, such as the prolonged educational period, that keep young people dependent on their parents more than is desirable. But the fact is that most fifteen- and sixteen-year-olds, disregarding for the moment those who have suffered infantilizing educational damage, could assume many times the responsibility for themselves and for their fellow associates that is granted them today. There are numerous instances of this in other cultures and in ours as well, especially among the many broken families of the war and post-war periods, in which young people showed how sensibly and intelligently they were able to perform heavy tasks with a greater degree of responsibility than has generally been expected from "half children." The practical importance of these cases, however, has been given little attention—as though they were simply irrelevant oddities. It has hardly penetrated the public consciousness that in reality there is a greater potential maturity in the young after puberty than can find expression in the social roles entrusted to them.

If parents today slowly venture to behave in a more liberal and permissive fashion toward their children, the last thing they should do is pose as greathearted benefactors whose generosity merits thanks, when what they are doing is showing elementary common sense. Families in the future will be able to do their best by their children up to and into the period of adolescence only if the young people are by that time able to make free and, insofar as possible, unsupervised use of the human relationships within the parental family; this helps to strengthen their identity. But it will be ever more dangerous, and in the end disastrous, if young people are forced to put up with certain limitations to their self-development made necessary by the educational process, as though they were performing a sort of "child's duty" instead of accepting such limitations freely. It is wrong to pretend that these limitations are natural and not highly unnatural, as in fact they are.

Parents must come to recognize, to their own relief, what an advantage there is in offering their children an equal partnership at an early age. This suggestion does not mean the irresponsible burdening of children with their parents' unresolved emotional disturbances—making them the scapegoats, for instance, or prodigies to redeem their parents' lack of success, or political companions-in-arms, or even semi-sexual partners, according to the nature of their parents' neuroses.[73] What is needed is a planned and progressive attempt to offer the children a chance to discuss openly and resolve together the common problems of the family. The psychotherapist always discovers that children know much more about their parents and their parents' difficulties than the parents suspect. They often intuit precisely the state of their parents' marriage. They know when their father is having business difficulties, when financial anxieties or rivalry with relatives weigh the atmosphere. They also often suspect that their parents hide their problems from them simply out of fear of the children's critical judgment. On that account alone, parents should not be surprised when the children for their part choose not to talk about their own difficulties. Each side protects itself from the other, and this attitude originates because the parents are filled with paranoid distrust and will not accept the implicit offer of partnership from their children. If parents had the sense and courage to recognize and accept this offer, there would be a far better atmosphere and true solidarity in the home; there would be an end to the concealments and play-acting and artificial intellectual isolation of the children that customarily go on far too long.

The surmise on the part of the parents that once there has been an open discussion of problems with their children, they can never again return to their role of unique and wonderful, godlike beings is certainly justified. In most cases, however, the children have already, years before, revised this picture of their parents in the interest of their own further development; only they have not said so, because the parents, out of fear of the altered image, wouldn't have listened to a word.

Another psychological problem for the family in a time of social change is a redefinition of the relation of the sexes. Contrary to the expectation of many, the progressive liberation of women has not resulted in the general breakup of marriages. What produced that has been primarily an alteration of the male role in the opposite direction. With the strengthening of the woman's position has gone, hand in hand, a weakening of the man's. When men visit a psychosomatic clinic or a marriage-counseling service because of marriage difficulties, we hear fewer complaints about the threatening claims of women than about their lack of active cooperation in the sharing of responsibility and the work load in the family. Thus it is dissatisfaction with too weak a woman rather than fear of too strong a woman that is now a problem for a relatively large number of men. The reverse is the basis of the complaints of many women, who feel that too much activity is expected of them by exhausted men seeking relaxation. Often the husband is felt to be like an eldest son—too demanding and, on the other hand, not sufficiently responsible.

There is good reason to believe that men have begun to express much more freely their need of passivity, long suppressed as disgraceful, and that this is partly responsible for the outburst of demands for women's liberation. Here prolonged reciprocal changes in orientation and adaptation are in progress whose outcome it is still hard to foresee.

There is a further development under way whose outcome is uncertain: Will families open themselves to wider contacts than ever before, or shut themselves off even more drastically? It is conceivable that the tendency toward communal living, or "big families" of people not necessarily related by blood or marriage, will grow, especially among the new generation. Many young people have found it an advantage to avoid the special dependency dangers of an early marriage or the exclusive union of a couple, without, on the other hand, having to be alone. The fear of surrender to a single individual, of being cut off from possibilities for the broader contacts needed for a free development of the self, apparently continues to play an ever increasing role. In itself, this is a welcome tendency to the psychoanalyst; a freer feeling in the relationship of couples and of the family toward the outside world would diminish the factors that in all strata of society have led to neurotic distortions of marriage and family structures. The interpretation of the partnership relation as one of ownership, with the resulting paranoidal fears of betrayal and loss of possession, had led and continues all too often to lead to an overrestrictive symbiotic clinging together, in which fear of separation and constant checks on the other's fidelity may smother positive feelings.

Learning to associate openly with one another in somewhat larger groups and to make use of the stimuli of such circles holds attraction for a growing number of people. Beyond question, moreover, the new psychotherapeutic technique of group therapy has found wide approval not only because it has objective therapeutic advantages but even more because the life style of such groups, similar to the "commune's," answers widespread needs. It is a tendency of our time to experiment with this kind of group structure in the areas of work and recreation. In any case, these developments are also significant for the future life style of the family.

One more observation about the special problems of women. As a result of the changing relationship of the sexes, it would appear that the increasing desire on the part of women for activity outside the home will in the long run encounter fewer obstacles from male fear of competition—though this has not yet disappeared—than from the duties of motherhood and housekeeping that intrude on women's desire for training and employment. A great many girls and women have learned how much inner security and self-assurance can be gained from successful training and even more so from professional competence. But only some of them can continue their professional careers without interruption after even a short leave for child care. Raising several children can make it impossible for a woman to continue her professional activity. In a number of specialized professions, a few years' interruption for homemaking is enough to reduce a woman's performance below the required standard. At the very least, in the more demanding callings special courage is required of a woman who, after several years of working at household duties, wishes to venture a second start and tries to make up for a considerable loss of accomplishment, knowing she has been outstripped by the competition of younger women. At all events, the anticipated difficulties of returning to a profession after having withdrawn completely into housekeeping frighten many young women enough so that they dare not try it. Here, however, progressive legislation could do a good deal to ease the reintegration of young mothers into their professions. In this, regulations in Soviet Russia, for example, are remarkably helpful; young mothers are provided there with an income during the period of child care and are assured of keeping their jobs.

The many women who, for a variety of reasons, definitely give up their professions in the interests of homemaking encounter, often for the first time as they grow older, serious difficulties in the role they are to play. During their younger years their identities have had substantial support from professional activity, but in time the curtailment of their social influence becomes a problem. Needed less and less by their maturing children, they become increasingly lonely. A day comes when, except for their husband, no one spontaneously offers them assurance that their activities have meaning, or has praise for their efforts, or even has a lively conversation to offer. Unless they have special interests of their own or form rewarding friendships, depressive feelings of emptiness, inferiority, and futility can easily become preponderant. This, then, can be seen as an individual psychopathological failing or, alternatively, as a marriage and family problem. For if the other members of the family are aware of the difficulty, they can point out new subjects of interest and new tasks to make better use of an aging woman's unsatisfied need for company and her ability to work.

This problem is related to the treatment of older people in general. By degrees, this subject has been receiving more sympathetic attention in our society. But it is still not being studied as deeply as it should be, and much about it is completely obscure. For a number of generations a remarkable disorientation and uncertainty have prevailed in our attitude toward the aged and what should be done about them. It is symptomatic that for a long time there has been, on the part of sociology, medicine, and psychology, a notable lack of research into the aging process. Even psychoanalysis has concerned itself only by exception, and only recently has it really taken up the problems of old age, now that psychoanalysts, contrary to earlier practice, are accepting a larger proportion of elderly patients for treatment.* The present advances in geriatrics and in the care of the aged within the framework of the mental-health movement seem to herald a change for the better; possibly we are on the verge of a rediscovery of the older generation. What sort of image will the aged present in the future, and what role can and will society assign them?

It is a trite, yet obviously not gratuitous, observation that, first of all, a more equitable regard for the interests of the aged, in contrast with those of the younger generation, must be achieved. Just as it seems of great importance that the young should more and more rid themselves of the harmful domination of their elders and that these elders should voluntarily give up their culturally deep-rooted tendency to misuse power, so on the other hand the young need a warning not to make in the future the mistakes they are struggling against now. The start of a possible wrong course is to be found in various pronouncements from radical circles, according to which the old are to be regarded simply as part-time handymen in the service of a

* Cf. G. L. Bibring: "Advanced Age, Passive and Active," *Psyche* 23 (1969), p. 262.

young, revolutionary generation. Unquestionably, such views, which are both one-sidedly defensive and repressive, are fed by unassimilated fear and a desire for retaliation. To combat this, one may hope for a growing realization that in fact the power of the old has already begun to disappear in many institutions (family, school, college, etc.) and may go on diminishing, so that an image of the older generations may emerge that is less distorted by apprehension and antagonism. In any case, it is clear that society in our rapidly changing world will understand and properly define the role of the aged only when it can see them as more than agents of reactionary repression or burdensome beings in need of social assistance or, finally, convenient screens on which to project excuses for society's failure.

Beyond question, the outcome of the identity crisis in young people will principally decide whether their generation can become more interested in living in cooperation instead of with a defensive-critical attitude vis-à-vis the preceding generation. By prolonged lingering in defiant, narcissistic isolation, as they widely choose to do today, young people give the elderly no adequate opportunity to find a meaningful role in their lives. A gradual relaxation of tension in the relationship of the generations might provide elderly people with new and satisfying tasks. The images of the tyrannical, miserly grandfather and the witch-like, wicked grandmother or mother-in-law are not timeless, dominant archetypes of the older generation but are to a large extent historically determined. It is entirely conceivable that the increasing activity of young women in the business world will result in the restoring to grandparents, especially grandmothers, a considerable part of the importance within the family of which they have for the time being been deprived. This may be helped along by the fact that young women, more self-assured because of their educational and professional accomplishments, will come to have less fear of being forced into a state of dependency if they maintain a close relationship with mother or mother-in-law. Even now, those with a mature self-confidence exact the consideration which the old must accustom themselves to give. The idea that a young family can be free only if alone and that any close relation with grandparents will result in subjection to them is of course connected with the unconscious fear of succumbing to the temptation to surrender oneself in passive childishness to the domination of one's elders. This inner danger regularly crops up in any case in which young married people provoke endless, seesawing problems of dependency and release with their parents or parents-in-law.

Another kind of trouble between a young family and the older generation appears when elderly people are unable to participate in any useful way with the young family and out of fear of isolation use established relationships of dependency to force continuation of a symbiotic relationship. Thus arise the typical neurotic family structures in which the grandparents strengthen through blackmail the inner uncertainty and guilt feelings of the young married pair, simply to avoid being driven out. Here one sees, for instance, the mother or mother-in-law who bitterly fights for her ideas for the education of the grandchildren, or the father or father-in-law who intrudes disturbingly instead of participating helpfully in the young family's living arrangements. The tyranny of helplessness and infirmity is often, of course, more dangerous than the tyranny of power. This is the case with old people who have found a way, through manipulation of guilt feelings, to defend their presence, sometimes even in a dominant role, in the young family's home. By continual allusions to their ill health and frailty, they imply a constant reproach as punishment on their children for their desire to be self-sufficient and separate. The plaint is repeatedly raised that this poor helpless old fellow must allow himself to be pushed around, that anyway he has not long to live, and that it will certainly be all right with the young people if by their impatient behavior they make that period even shorter. Reference to the grave at whose edge the children one day will perhaps repent their selfishness is usually the final trump in this grotesque but too frequently successful strategy.

These traditional maneuvers of intimidation, born originally of fear of isolation, may gradually lose their effectiveness on a generation of more self-assured, more emancipated young people who will counter these moves with further withdrawal rather than submission. The old people must in any case learn that social

change reduces their chances of remaining as relatively functionless objects of care in families that are overtaxed by these
responsibilities. In favorable circumstances, a family can sustain
such a burden, but many other families are overly strained by it,
especially if the younger woman is forced to give up her position
in business to take over the care of the aged in the household.

The home for the aged, once despised and feared as a dismal
institution of detention, is gradually assuming a new aspect
and a better reputation. Society is slowly learning that old
people's homes should not be places where those who have
been thrown out or are without relatives wait for death; by
intelligent arrangements, they must be made so attractive that
old people can pursue their interests there in a positive way.
The typical apathetic, dozing inmate is to a large extent the
artificial product of a society that has brought about such empty
lives through its repulsive, barren institutions. Today one sees
that old people in properly organized homes behave in a much
more enterprising and socially outgoing fashion than those in
the older establishments. A stimulating environment shows what
an astounding amount of dynamism, of impulse and interest
there still is during this late phase of life. And it is highly significant that this dynamism in a well-conducted home for the
aged can develop in a more lively way than in a family where
an old person sees himself as a useless bystander, barely
tolerated and required to subordinate himself entirely to the
interests of the younger people. In the well-run home for the
aged, the old person joins a group with problems like his own.
He is not the only frail one among the young and strong; many
around him are feebler than he. So he is once more in a group
in which he can keep step, and this alone can repair much of
his damaged self-esteem. Also, there are opportunities for ex-
changing sentiments and for establishing stimulating partnerships which an old person isolated from his contemporaries
would probably not have thought possible.

In any case, it will be most helpful if homes for older people
can offer a really attractive alternative, something society can
provide without feeling guilty. It will be a much better solution
for many families in which an aged, infirm person feels that he

is a worthless fifth wheel and is tolerated by his relatives only out of compassion. A situation of this sort, tormenting to all involved, is taken as a lesser evil than the opprobrium of the old people's home—a concept now rendered invalid by the existence of better institutions for the homeless.

This has been no more than a sketch outline of some of the difficulties as well as some of the hopes that the psychotherapist considers typical of families in process of change. Every case that confronts the therapist is rooted in this kind of social nexus, whose detailed clarification and objective description are the business of the family sociologist. On the other hand, sociological considerations and discoveries have limited usefulness for the psychotherapist. Regardless of sociological statements about the role and function of the family and its members in today's society, wholly atypical individual factors in an individual family may become relevant for the therapist. He sees, in addition to conflicts which are more or less characteristic of the sociological background of a family, many conflicts in which the personal psychodynamism of those involved predominates. Despite the similar characteristics of sociological roles, individuals and families vary through a wide scale of psychological possibilities. The family sociologist, therefore, cannot provide binding therapeutic precepts. Each family reflects in its own specific way the influence of the sociocultural milieu at work upon it. And its specific problem is dependent upon psychodynamic factors that must be individually diagnosed each time if one wishes to establish successful therapeutic communication. This will be illustrated in later chapters by various case histories intended to make clear the operation of family psychotherapy.

3

On the Psychoanalytical Theory
of Family Conflicts

Because from the very beginning of psychoanalytical theory the Oedipus complex has been a primary subject of discussion, one might imagine that psychoanalysis has been constantly concerned with the origin and structure of family conflicts.

Freud and his disciples pursued in great detail the way in which the child, through the oral, anal, and genital phases of its development, formed specific relationships, first with its mother, then with both parents, then with brothers and sisters, and later with other partners, and what problems these relationships created. Numerous investigations by Freud raised such questions as: What needs does a child have to have fulfilled by his parents at what period? How does the child, through association with his parents, bring about the differentiation of his own character? How does a psychopathological disturbance of childhood development occur through complication of these intrafamily relationships?

All this is more than psychology of the individual; it embraces family psychology. Yet Freud's approach was not really sociopsychological. His whole grand psychoanalytic doctrine of development is based fundamentally on the individual conceptual model of his age, which also formed the basis of somatic medicine. The child with his requirements, which differ from phase to phase, stands at the center, and the members of his family are reduced to objects toward which he can direct his impulses, objects which serve as models in his need for identification— necessary models for the building up of his ego and his super- ego—and finally, as a result of the primal scene, help in the formation and subsidence of his Oedipus complex. In exchanges between members of the family and the child, what parents and brothers and sisters do to the child to satisfy their own uncon- scious and conscious needs receives only scant attention. Inso- far as Freud, for example, describes the effects of the mother on the child, he cites, almost exclusively, stereotyped factors which result automatically from the role of mother: he shows how the mother influences the child by quieting it or arousing it and finally by bringing a sibling rival into the world. He shows what effect the discovery that she has no penis can have on the boy child. Equally pallid and generalized is the picture of the father in Freud's family gallery. The father's share in the development of the boy's Oedipus complex, for example, is represented something like this: the father, simply as father, is great and powerful and places himself at the disposal of his son, who in the positive form of the Oedipus complex wants to be his rival and in the negative form wants to be loved by him. In this concept of relationships, mother and father are not persons whose individual expectations, wishes, and anxieties may help to shape the child's Oedipus complex.

Freud, to be sure, represents the parents not simply in their biologically determined generic characteristics but also as transmitters of the prevailing code of values. In this capacity the parents have a modifying effect on the ego-function of the child and they determine the content of the child's superego. They demand that the child's impulses be culturally acceptable. But even this sociological aspect of Freud's psychoanalytical method hardly leaves room for an understanding of the parents' relations with the child. The social standards transmitted by the parents appear in Freud almost as firmly fixed as the rule of natural law. To be sure, the origins of prehistoric and many historical social regulations are explained through analysis of motivations. But the Freudian social order as transmitted by parents is seemingly frozen into rigidity, almost like the unalterable biological reality of sexual differences or the ambivalence of instincts. So, not only are social standards unchangeable, but—and here a failure to apply psychoanalytical methods makes itself conspicuous—the parents as agents of society are portrayed as stereotypes and as completely inflexible. From the earlier psychoanalytical theory of development, one can easily get the impression that only the child is capable of discriminating, variable, psychic reactions and that the parents are wholly impersonal bearers of biological, generic characteristics (large or small, with or without breasts, with or without a penis) and play roles that are wholly socially determined.

The older clinical psychoanalytical literature, by limiting its view to the patient on principle, left the patients' relatives for the most part standing in the wings as subsidiary personages. They were frequently characterized as if they were aspects of the weather: cold, warm, severe, mild, gentle, hard, or the like; or perhaps from an economic point of view, as overindulgent, as affording emotional support, satisfying needs, or on the contrary as rejecting or frustrating the patient. Thus, the description of the world around the patient followed the conceptual model set by somatic medicine. This too, with a quite different justification, concentrated on the individual organism, whose life processes are determined by external factors such as air pressure, temperature, oxygen, water, sources of nourishment, and microorganisms. But it is easy to see that characteristics of the environment that are meaningful in organic medicine are inappropriate in psychological medicine. In the psychological realm the patient is, first of all, involved with other people and not primarily with his biochemical or biophysical surroundings.

Nevertheless, the description of the inner psychic functioning of the individual as if modeled on somatic medicine was probably an essential methodical prerequisite for working out the comprehensive view of the development, structure, and dynamic processes of the individual's psychic mechanism, and for this we are indebted to Freud. As a matter of fact, the extension of the strict psychoanalytical view to group processes implies that the intra-individual structure and laws of behavior are known first. Only then can there be an examination and description of the interaction which results from the mingling of the unconsciously determined desires, fears, and defense mechanisms between individuals. Whatever symptomatic superstructure may be found in group processes does not result in eliminating or weakening those intra-individual determinants that Freud discovered; the important thing is, rather, to understand their reciprocal interplay. In this sense it is unquestionably time to widen the sociopsychological purview of psychological medicine. And let it once more be strongly emphasized that this should be done by extending psychoanalytical thinking to the social sphere. There is no reason whatever to expect that a simplification of social factors will solve psychosocial conflicts and put an end to symptom formation, eliminating the need for the depth and subtlety of psychoanalytical research into motivation. On the contrary, the hitherto usual external and formal descriptions of social interaction, which psychological medicine plainly should devote more attention to, must be studied for their manifold motivations and without any simplification of the psychoanalytical approach. A synthesis of psychoanalysis and social research in the sense of introducing overall social forces (which influence only the conscious level and not the unconscious), as psychological determinants—thus far we can agree with a recent statement by Adorno—is in fact of no advantage.[3]

Rapidly though the literature on the relationship between family dynamics and psychogenic disturbances is growing (Ackerman[1, 2]; Ehrenwald[22]; Jackson[52]; Lidz[60, 62, 63]; Pollock[68]; Singer and Wynne[86]; Boszormenyi-Nagy[10]; Grotjahn[44]), we still lack a discriminative, convincing model for understanding the process of interchange between individuals and the forms of its disturbance, such as we have, thanks to Freud, for the intra-individual processes. When we want to understand the dynamics of an individual neurosis, we know exactly how to proceed. We characterize the conflict, for instance, by determining what impulses are being inhibited, through what mechanisms, on what level of fixation, with what formation of the superego, and with what symptomatic results. But how, theoretically, is one to deal with the content of a disturbance in which two or more persons are involved as partners?

Oversimplified categories have often been considered sufficient for the understanding of social relationships within the family, categories that should be rated as a step backward into preanalytical thinking. In such categories it is determined that one person accepts or rejects the other, that one inhibits or demands too much of the other, that the partners have proved ambivalent toward each other, etc. In individual cases these may be important characteristics, but they are extremely general and by comparison with the highly differentiated possibilities of describing individual structures, they do not by any means explore deeply enough the dynamic complexity of a partner relationship.

Recently we have had various suggestions intended to make possible the understanding of emotional interactions within the family and the conflicts that may result from them. There is Jackson's concept of family homeostasis,[52] and Weakland,[93] from the same group of workers in Palo Alto, has recently proposed a model for two- and three-person conflicts based on communications principles, which has become known as the "double-bind" theory. He has attempted to prove its usefulness through the findings obtained by Lidz in schizophrenic families. Wallace and Fogelson[91] have developed from Erikson's identity concept a theory of interaction that they call "identity struggle." This model is directed toward the understanding of two-person conflicts and in many respects resembles Wynne's[86, 95] concept of "trading dissociations." By this formula Wynne means that each person holds at bay the symptoms that seem threatening in himself by localizing them, as it were, in the other person, with the aid of an unconscious dissociation procedure. In addition, Wynne and Singer[86] as well as Lidz[60, 62, 63] have formulated a flexible hypothesis about the disturbances of thinking and communication between parents and children, which has proved a suitable basis for fruitful experimental investigations in families of schizophrenics. I myself have sought to introduce a role theory for the parent-child relationship, to provide a systematic understanding of the psychosocial forms of defense classified according to the nature of the role played. This role theory was originally developed simply for the parent-child relationship; however, it can be applied to partner relationships among adults as well.

We begin by making use of the basic types of partnership choice (object-choice) described by Freud. "Role" is here defined as the organized totality of the unconscious and conscious expectations that the partners have of each other. These roles can serve predominantly or entirely as defense processes. This means that the bestowing or accepting of these prescribed roles serves to free each of the partners, in compensation, from the tension of his own inner conflict. (The mechanism of compensating roles is normal enough in partner relationships; it is only when they reach an exaggerated form that they are psychologically hazardous.) Instead of acknowledging personal conflicts and working them out, those concerned bring them into the partner relationship and make use of the partner of the moment as a compensatory substitute object or as the narcissistic extension of themselves. In this sense, the reciprocally allotted roles become identical with the basic forms of psychosocial defense. They are maneuvers in the partner relationship that have the same purpose as the long-recognized intra-individual defense mechanisms: they provide an escape from unbearable inner conflicts. However, these psychosocial defense formations do not come as additions to the classical defense mechanisms, as classified by Anna Freud, but constitute superstructures. The classical mechanisms are always part of the psychosocial defense formations. They make possible their development in the first place, but in the sociopsychological context they take on a new, overriding significance.

The prescribed roles, which have been fully described and illustrated by examples elsewhere, can be classified as follows:

1. *Role of Partner Substitute*

Y can be unconsciously compelled by X to assume the role of proxy for a former partner of X's (Z); Z is usually someone in X's infancy with whom there was conflict that is now a trauma in X's unconscious. Y is then supposed to compensate for the unbearable disillusionment left behind by that other unfulfilled or broken relationship with Z. At the same time, however, Y out of subconscious repetition compulsion is led to reproduce exactly the same traumatizing characteristics under pressure of which the original partner conflicts with Z became psychically fixated. Depending on circumstances, the role of Y will be that of a pre-Oedipal or Oedipal father image or that of a sibling.

2. *Role of Duplicate*

Y can have thrust upon him the role of playing an exact copy of X's self-image. The X who allots this prescribed role is always a highly developed, narcissistic personality with paranoid traits, who through disowning his real ego-ideal achieves the fantasy of being perfect. Naturally, it takes great effort to maintain a narcissistic, perfectionist fantasy in a world that constantly emphasizes the illusory nature of self-inflation. Under no circumstances must Y acknowledge the precepts and ideals whose persistent denial demands enormous effort from X. For if Y were not to join in that denial he would be a constant threat to X's defense system and would evoke fear.

3. *Role of Ideal Self*

In this case, Y is compelled in narcissistic fashion to fulfill an ideal that X has failed to achieve. Thus Y becomes in a sense the substitute for X's ideal self. This prescribed role presupposes that X is not able to maintain the fantasy of his own omnipotent perfection through paranoid concealment but is suffering from the failure of his ego-ideal. For this reason, he not only tolerates Y's being "better" than himself but actually demands it, in order, through narcissistic identification, to gain compensation for his own failure. In this narcissistic way he obtains "healing through love," as Freud called it in *On Narcissism: An Introduction*.[30] This role can differ in content, depending on whether X imposes upon Y more of the positive wish-fulfillment aspect of his own ego-ideal or the negative, repressive aspect of his superego (Giltay,[39] Lampl de Groot[57]). In the first case, what is demanded of Y is, for example, conspicuous cleverness, success, beauty, reputation; in the second instance, perhaps, the fulfillment of an ideal of absolute purity, abstinence, or the like.

4. *Role of Negative Self*

Finally, Y can be compelled by X to "take over" the latter's negative side. Thus Y must represent an aspect which X can successfully repress and disclaim in himself only by imposing it to a certain extent upon Y. Y thereupon becomes an incarnation of X's negative identity. In overt sadomasochistic forms of this combination of roles, Y becomes the scapegoat.

a) *The Scapegoat's Role*

Here Y must carry out the especially dangerous impulses that X despises in himself and represses; at the same time, Y must stand ready to receive the punishment, thus relieving X of what he secretly believes he himself deserves. And so, as scapegoat, Y provides X on the one hand with a guiltless substitute satisfaction for his own repressed impulses (that is, through imaginary participation) and on the other hand makes it possible for X to get rid of his tormenting impulses toward self-punishment. In contrast to the role described in 3 (substitute for the ideal self), this time instead of talking about an attempt to heal oneself through love, one would have to call it an attempt to heal through hate. In such a case, X is always a person with very little control over his instincts; he can keep them tolerably in check only because he can voyeuristically satisfy them through participation in the sensual exploits to which he disastrously incites Y and which he knows how to repudiate in his own eyes and those of the world by periodic excessive punishments of Y.

Whereas in the scapegoat variation of this role the sadomasochistic relationship predominates, this is not as true of the following pattern.

b) *Role of Weaker Part*

In this role, Y must take over not the wicked but only the weak part of X. X can present himself as great, strong, and energetic as long as his repressed conviction of unimportance, weakness, and passivity finds expression in his symbiotic partner, Y. It can then be said that Y expresses the depression that X defends himself against. Y is the helpless reverse side which X in his phallic, narcissistic self-representation conceals by overcompensating. If X were compelled to see this weak side of himself, he would find his manic, narcissistic self-importance badly shattered, but as long as Y accepts the depressed aspect, X can feel safe. Poor weak Y allows X to shine unchallenged in all his greatness. At the same time, however, X can secretly enjoy a part of his own repressed passivity and depression in his symbiotic love for Y. Though a psychologically inexperienced observer may think that in these cases Y must be simply a crushing burden for X, unconsciously X derives from this combination of roles—often unnoticed by those around—sufficient compensation.

5. Role of Ally

X constantly carries on battles with outsiders and demands from his partner Y, above all, the services of an ally. Everything else that Y is and does is trivial in comparison with his importance as comrade-in-arms. This role looks like an extreme variant of role 2 (role of duplicate). In it, too, one must presuppose a paranoid structure on the part of X, who assigned the roles. But this time what is important to X is less the concealment of his narcissistic deception than a reliable way of discharging his aggressions. The appeal to be a comrade-in-arms easily becomes an inescapable compulsion for Y. Were his bellicose solidarity with X to disappear, X's aggression, which has been kept out of the partner relationship, would threaten to break in, with destructive consequences. This explains, for example, why those married to paranoid persons enter into their partner's delusions and often become allies in their paranoid battles.

The tabular classification of prescribed roles cannot be reproduced here as completely or in as much detail as has already been done in another book,* where it is expounded and illustrated with ample case histories. However, it must be

* Horst E. Richter: *Eltern, Kind und Neurose. Psychoanalyse der kindlichen Rolle*, Stuttgart, 1963; Reinbek, 1969.

stressed once more that these interrelated roles represent, with only slight exaggeration, normal admixtures in the emotional attitudes of partners to each other. They are present everywhere. But as soon as the prescribed roles take on a dominant significance for the behavior of one of the partners, they become abnormal in character. Then they serve a defensive purpose for that person. Under pressure of fear, he achieves a partial compromise solution of his inner conflicts. Thus the demands on the partner who plays the various roles assume, as we have said, the meaning of psychosocial defenses, in many respects fulfilling a function similar to the recognized intra-individual defense mechanisms classified by Anna Freud.[27] These classical mechanisms, such as repression, regression, projection, introjection, reaction formation, displacement, etc., are always at work in the configuration of the interrelated roles just described. From a sociopsychological point of view, they are simply functioning in a new sense, with overwhelming complexity.

One of the ways these psychosocial forms of defense, leading to the above-mentioned roles, can be identified is that they result not only in the displacement of the inner balance of the individual but in a direct bipolar or even multipolar summing up of the group situation. Even if one sticks to the simplified model according to which a partner relationship is entirely organized and directed by the dominant party, nevertheless this script contains here and there a part for each of the individuals involved in the play. If the director is seeking a protective mother, he promptly turns himself into a helpless child. If he creates a scapegoat, then he is claiming for himself the position of righteous prosecutor; if he cultivates a sadist for himself, then he wants to play the part of masochistic whipping boy. Thus this conception of theoretical roles opens up a multiple approach to group problems, in contrast to the traditional approach focused on the individual, in which one person is regarded as having functions and instincts, whereas his partner seems ultimately to be little more than a sounding board for these positive or negative impulses.

Among the partner relationships that emerge from the predominance of one or another of these typical roles, a distinction can be made between the asymmetrical and the symmetrical structures. In an asymmetrical structure it is predominantly one partner who forcibly compels the other to stay in a compensatory role, whereas in the symmetrical configuration interest in supporting the interrelated roles is fairly evenly divided between the two partners.

It would be wrong to assume that symmetrical relationships of this sort are to be found, at most, among adults and not between parent and child. The fact is that a distortion of roles between parent and child regularly results from the overpowering parental figure imposing upon the child a role necessary for the parent's own escape from inner conflict. But if the child accepts his part and the transposed roles work for a while, the prescribed complementary role reflected back from the child to the parent may one day attain the same intensity of demand that the child himself was originally subjected to. Indeed, not infrequently a reversal takes place in the sense that the child insists on maintaining the now-established role relationship, which the parent needed only temporarily and imposed as a way of escape from his own conflicts.

It is easy to make a mistake about the symmetry structure of the compensatory relationship if one simply compares the partners in a superficial behavioristic way in respect to their overt "activity" or "energy." In a mother-daughter relationship, for instance, in which the mother exercises massive overprotection and the twenty-year-old daughter plays a helpless, ailing child, the mother naturally seems to be the guiding and principally responsible party in the distorted relationship. Just as clearly, an overt sadist appears to be the guilty tormentor of his timid, woebegone, masochistic partner. Psychoanalytic experience, however, shows that overt vigor and bombastic behavior are by no means reliable criteria for determining which of the partners actually holds the other more forcibly in the prison of his compensatory role. Usually, only a thorough psychoanalytical investigation will produce an answer to this question—and quite often to the disadvantage of the apparently weaker, downtrodden, "inhibited" partner.

But sometimes it is hardly possible (and also of no help in

developing the therapeutic transference) to determine the degree of dominance in such compensatory roles or to give the question primary importance. It is difficult to compare the intensity of heterogeneous approaches, as for instance in massive sadistic activity and quiet reproachful suffering. Very often one would be right in accepting a rough dovetailing of roles. Thus director and directed can be seen bound to each other: dejected depressives and manic megalomaniacs; savage tyrants and passive slaves; but also paranoid narcissists as like to each other as two eggs. Each needs the other in the same way—and seeks frantically for a substitute if his partner becomes unavailable to play the compensatory role. At any rate, one sees instances of equilibrium in which the individual conflicts and the resulting roles demanded by each partner fit together with absolute precision. If, in these cases, one analyzes closely the ego structure of the partners, one discovers with surprise and dismay that each has become identified unconsciously and perhaps very firmly with existence as a "partial person" who has to be supplemented by the other, compensatory person. One is reminded of the Platonic myth of the two separate halves of an original whole striving to reunite, when one learns what an extreme degree of unconscious reciprocal dependence arises in such partner relations. In the end, neither partner is able—down to the unconscious depths of his ego identity—to understand himself as a whole person or even to attempt to attain a personal self. Each is not only content with this situation but is anxiously intent upon maintaining himself as the torso of a personality, thereby remaining absolutely dependent for his viability on a supplementary person.

4

The Structure of Family Neuroses
SYMPTOM NEUROSES AND CHARACTER NEUROSES

The discovery of the close psychic dependency that prevails in many families complicates the problems of description and diagnosis in psychological medicine. A psychic disturbance is not exclusively the concern of the stricken individual but may have to do principally with the family as a whole. Many psychogenic disturbances can be effectively grasped only when they are seen not as individual illnesses but as marriage or family neuroses.

This approach is unfamiliar and at the moment it does not fit into our firmly established system of medical organization. Hitherto, doctors, health-insurance companies, and income-insurance agencies have recognized only the individual patient. And for somatic medicine there is no good reason to change this view. But psychological medicine no longer makes sense simply as individual medicine, even though for reasons of prestige it would like to amalgamate still more closely with organized medicine, in order to emerge from its twilight status as an outsider and incorporate itself fully into the socioeconomic system of medicine as a whole.

Among family neurotic disturbances, two types can be distinguished:

1. *Family symptom neuroses*
2. *Family character neuroses*

In a *family symptom neurosis,* the family or sometimes a part of it makes one of its members (occasionally more than one) sick and treats him as a "case." Powerful pressure is exerted on this individual until he cannot cope, usually with accompanying medical symptoms, sometimes too with signs of demoralization. Thus the rest of the family provide themselves with a release by inducing their "victim's" breakdown. Just as a conversion hysteric can drain off part of the tension of his unresolved conflict through a localized conversion symptom, so a neurotic family can drain away part of its internal group tension by producing a manifest disturbance in a convenient member. One might then describe this member as the family's "local symptom."[74] At the moment when this individual falls ill or becomes socially objectionable, there ensues a remarkable calm in the formerly excited family atmosphere. In particular, there is often a marked relaxation in the tension between the symptom bearer and the person closest to him. Paradoxically, it often turns out that it is the family member who seems healthiest whose pressure produces illness in another part of the family. Oberndorf,[65] who experimented very early with the simultaneous psychoanalysis of husband and wife, mentions this type of interaction as early as 1933: "The inductor in neurotic familial situations is often the individual who considers himself and is often considered the normal person." In 1944 Mittelmann[64] described partnerships "in which the needs of one individual are satisfied and his anxiety kept at a minimum by the behavior of the other who, in turn, is satisfied only in part while many of his cravings remain unsatisfied and his anxiety is aroused. Thus one individual appears well whereas the other is manifestly sick."

In this way, one part of the family escapes an outbreak of neurotic illness by imposing its unsolved problems upon another part. This compensatory division of roles is demonstrated by the fact that, repeatedly, the therapeutic improvement of a neurotic person may lead to the appearance of symptoms or the increased severity of symptoms in someone close to him. The presence of a partner who is defeated by problems one denies in oneself can in any case sometimes temporarily free one from

the pressure of one's own conflict. If, however, the externaliza-
tion of the unresolved problems becomes impossible because
the compensatory partner has been cured, then the equilibrium
of the apparently healthy person collapses. He now falls victim
to the difficulties from which he had formerly been relieved by
the other.

It is characteristic of the symptom-neurotic family that a
division takes place within it. That part of the family which
develops symptoms or is socially unacceptable is isolated by the
others. The "victim" is more or less isolated within the family.
In flagrant cases it comes to actual expulsion. Fleck[26] speaks in
this case of "the ejecting type of family."

Both parents periodically direct at one of their children their
unresolved marital tension, to the accompaniment of joint
cannonades of abuse and a variety of punishments, until the
child becomes more and more depressed and runs away several
times. Finally, he has to be sent to a home. The parents then
immediately repeat the whipping-boy tactics with a second child.
This one, too, presently succumbs to the crushing aggression of
his parents, develops a chronic stomach disorder, and is sent to
the hospital.

In institutions for educational counseling, one encounters
families which expel a member every few years; one divorce
follows another, a child lands in a home, a second in the
hospital, a third attempts suicide. Closer psychoanalytical observation usually reveals that under pressure from a violently
active sociopath, forcible ejection from the family is attempted
again and again as the simplest solution for strongly aggressive
group conflicts.

Less striking and also less radical is the action of many
families which maneuver several members, one after another,
into the position of outsider, without attempting actual expulsion. The "victim" is chivied into the position of a do-nothing
among energetic persons, a bad-luck Johnny among the successful, a sick man among the well, a faintheart among the confident. The other members of the family use the virtually un-
resisting partner as a screen on which to project their own
unacknowledged defects, but they keep him firmly within the

family to fulfill this function. The rest of the family feels collectively "different" from the isolated victim. They feel better, stronger, healthier—because they have deposited on their ostracized member their own disavowed notion of guilt, their feelings of impotence and insufficiency. But because he is a defenseless storehouse and at the same time a safety valve, the symptom bearer is so important to the rest of the family that they are deeply concerned to keep him in his role. He is nursed and coddled in a kind of golden cage. In some instances, he is taken to see a number of doctors and even perhaps exposed to a psychotherapist. To be sure, the sort of psychotherapist is chosen who will work on the symptoms of the patient and leave his slavery within the family untouched. The case history in chapter 13 gives a striking example of how psychiatrists and psychotherapists can, more or less unperceived, become active participants in stabilizing this kind of family neurosis.

In contrast to the family symptom neurosis, the *family character neurosis* occurs when the "collective ego" of the family undergoes a change under the pressure of an unresolved conflict. The family builds itself a neurotic world, often with the aid of an ideology, which in some way serves to compensate for the inner tension of the neurotic family conflict.

The distinguishing mark of a family character neurosis is that no expulsion or other discriminatory isolation of the symptom bearer occurs. In general, the family suffering from a character neurosis does not consist of two parts—one healthy, one sick—but gradually forms an ensemble of remarkable uniformity.

This ensemble is maintained, indeed sometimes even strengthened in its solidarity, if a member of the family becomes manifestly ill. The symptom bearer in a character-neurotic family is as a rule no outsider, or is not under reproach and threatened with rejection, but is rather a guiding member of the family group. The rest tend to overidentify with him. This can go to the extent of reinterpreting the family symptoms as the expression of something of great value and can be made the core of a paranoid ideology.

The real sickness of the character-neurotic family is that it creates an insane world for itself. A change occurs in its inner "nature." It establishes an egosyntonic system of values which, seen from the outside, is badly distorted. This "madness" originated and is sustained through the influence of that member of the family who is sickest. He would immediately break down if he did not succeed in falsifying the picture of reality for himself and for the rest of the family sufficiently to preserve his own inner equilibrium.

You could say that before the creation of a character neurosis the family felt it must choose one of two ways. It must either maintain its normal relationship to reality, at the cost of allowing its potentially most threatened member to go to pieces; or sacrifice its normal relationship to reality in the interest of a tension-free solidarity with the potential patient. It chose the second way.

Families with marked systematic character neuroses remind the outside observer of a family on Christmas Eve when everybody pretends to a child that they believe in Santa Claus bringing gifts. Or those families which at the deathbed of a cancer patient stage a play full of cheerful observations, in order to spare him and themselves a confrontation with terrifying reality. The essential difference is that the character-neurotic family, though possibly at the beginning it retains some awareness of the illusionary motive of its play, in the later phases is less and less aware of it. The examples in the following chapters will make clear how the different types of character-neurotic family in the end assimilate fully and without criticism their once consciously falsified picture of reality: the anxiety-neurotic family believes in a world resembling a peaceful *sanitarium;* the paranoid family sees all its problems as though through the embrasures of its imaginary *fortress*; and the hysterical family turns the whole world, in fantasy, into a *theater*.

Now one might think that a family with this kind of limited or distorted vision of reality would have to isolate itself from society. But this assumption is not always accurate. Character-neurotic changes in the "group ego" frequently take place in outside society too. Under the influence of a collective trend, many families may orient themselves at the same time to a neurotic alteration of their concept of reality. There is much evidence, for instance, that at the present time social circumstances favor the anxiety-neurotic family type. That is to say, many families, by means of avoidance and denial tactics, cling to the illusion of a peaceful, good, well-ordered world, in order to spare themselves the terrifying confrontation with existing social conflict and injustice. This will be discussed later in connection with a systematic description of the anxiety-neurotic family (chapter 6).

One is quite justified, then, in saying that an individual character neurosis is conspicuous only when it appears as a relative exception. As part of an epidemic of some particular character-neurotic transformation, it becomes simply the norm. And the family that is healthy from a psychoanalytical point of view may in the end appear as an offensive problem case against which society will erect a barrier of prejudice.

5

*Examples of Family Symptom Neuroses**

Symptom-neurotic families have to turn one or another of their members into a failure (either in the medical or the social sense) in order to put an end to the tensions within the group. If we disregard the cases in which members are expelled, we can distinguish families with constant symptom-bearers from those with alternating symptom-bearers. In the former, the family again and again makes use of the same person as safety valve. In the latter, one sees social symptom transference[76] within the family: a member originally picked out to be the symptom bearer gets well, and immediately another falls ill in his place. The role of failure is indispensable. If one person escapes from it, another is made ready to play the part, because without it the family cannot maintain its neurotically unstable balance.

In one family a whole series of social symptom transferences occurred, with one member after another going into psychotherapy. This resulted from the family habit of irritating one another and reciprocally heightening their neurotic conflicts.

* The family biographies and case histories contained in this book have been disguised to prevent identification.

Finally, there was only one little girl left who felt healthy and got along well in the group. She, so it seemed, could be spared psychotherapy. However, by degrees she became the goal of concerted attacks by the other persons in the family; they handed on to her in provocative fashion the insights they had received in their psychotherapeutic sessions, having discovered what a penetrating effect analytical interpretations can have. And it gave them satisfaction to attack the enviably healthy girl with the weapons to which they had been so painfully exposed in psychotherapy. Thereby, they set in motion the defense mechanism known as "identification with the aggressor."[27] Here is a deadly example. One day the children's mother did not return at the expected time from a shopping trip to the city. The girl expressed concern at her mother's lateness—whereupon her older brother said: "If you are afraid something has happened to Mother, it means you unconsciously wish for her death. You're full of repressed aggressions against your mother!" The girl's brothers and sisters accused her unrelentingly until she too broke down and required treatment. It was only then that she was left temporarily in peace.

In cases of this sort, various members of the family or the family as a whole join in harrying one of its members like a pack of dogs and finally make him ill. In other families, however, such processes go on principally between two persons, the remaining members acting chiefly as bystanders. A marital conflict may result in one of the partners being forced into the role of symptom bearer, while the children do little more than acquiesce in this arrangement and possibly help a little to fixate it.

"I liked you better when you were depressed!"

A very sensitive but ambitious and strong-willed advertising woman marries a schoolmaster older than herself. Having been constantly rejected and neglected by her own cold and tyrannical mother, she feels especially attracted by the emotional warmth and gentleness of her husband, who, she thinks, will give her the security she failed to get from her mother. She underestimates the fact that her husband, for all his tenderness, is badly spoiled and rather vain. He is clever at arranging things so that his mild manners appear magnanimous and he is praised to the skies. At his school he is constantly surrounded by a circle of worshipful and enamored schoolgirls. The wife, who at the time of the marriage was still, like the ecstatic schoolgirls, very unsure of herself, in the course of a ten-year marriage becomes an egocentric and headstrong partner, no longer fascinated by the husband's vain airs but on the contrary challenged by him. She becomes his bitter rival and cannot keep from attacking at every turn his essentially harmless illusions of grandeur as though they were proof of perfidious malice on his part. His self-confidence shaken, the husband tries to defend himself, but with his gentle temperament and essentially melancholic leanings, he cannot exist in an unfriendly atmosphere and quickly loses ground to the wife. Having resigned the leading role to her, he becomes querulous and morose, now in his turn attempting to belittle his wife's success out of envy. He feels he cannot forgo this revenge for the humiliation he has suffered. Meanwhile, his more robust wife pitilessly exploits his emotional instability. She precipitates arguments and compels him time and again to give in. His inner dependence on her inevitably places him in a masochistic position. Finally, he has to put up with her domineering manner even in the presence of others. She conspires with his colleagues at the school and undermines his reputation there through petty, hysterical intrigues.

During this unedifying battle for power, the husband and wife simultaneously compete for the favor of their two children, with unequal success. Both children had especially loved their cheerful, considerate father. But now they often find him a nag and behaving unreasonably. In his increasingly depressed mood, he is no longer able to treat his children with constant patience and encouragement. Instead, he alternates between affectionate indulgence and sudden irritable outbursts. The mother, on the other hand, formerly severe and short-tempered, now intentionally gives the children more freedom of action and a long-withheld measure of attention. And she succeeds in bringing them to rely on her as the obviously stronger, more dependable, more reasonable parent. Irritated by the weakness and unpredictability of their father, the children unconsciously abet their mother's tactics of progressively isolating him and depriving him of the courage to maintain his phallic-narcissistic role. But since playing this part was the protective device by which he had hitherto repressed his latent subterranean depression, there now ensues an inevitable breakdown. He falls ill with a severe reactive depression, becomes unbearable at home, and has to be sent to a neurological clinic.

After some months, he returns from the clinic. For the time being, the depression has been overcome, and he appears confident and high-spirited. His earlier mood of enterprise returns and he throws himself optimistically into his teaching activities. And it seems as though he could also assert himself better at home and win back some of his earlier importance in the family. But this disquiets the wife. During his illness she behaved helpfully and understandingly. The rivalry conflict seemed at an end, but now it breaks out anew. The energetic activities of the husband threaten her dominant role, which she believes firm as a rock. Her superficially repressed rivalry complex compels her to attack the barely mended self-confidence of her husband through renewed sneers, though her motivation, to be sure, is largely unconscious. She rationalizes her reproaches and attempts at intimidation by the argument that her husband ought not to forget that he recently suffered a serious nervous illness and now he should not be "too full of himself." If he attempts too much, he may easily suffer a relapse. At first, the husband seems sufficiently resilient and self-assured to withstand these irritations. But then the wife increases the pressure, provokes open arguments, and repeatedly betrays herself by expressions such as: "I liked you much better when you were depressed. Now I find you intolerable." Or: "Probably you'll have to get sick again to realize that I'm right." "If you go on acting this way, you'll soon have a relapse. And then you'll understand how unreasonably you've been behaving!" Thus she clearly reveals her preference that he be weak and neurotic once more rather than strong and able to compete with her. And in line with this preference, she actually prepares him for a new depressive breakdown. She criticizes him, sneers at him, denies his desire for sexual intercourse, and lets him wait for days if after some argument he begs for a reconciliation. In this way she systematically destroys the basis of his uncertain emotional equilibrium until he once more becomes anxious, uncertain, and pessimistic. Finally, he can hardly sleep at all, loses all impulse to activity, and slips into a second depressive illness. Once more, treatment in a neurological clinic is necessary.

This cycle is repeated twice more. In the neurological clinic the diagnosis is "cyclic endogenic depression." Meanwhile, as a result of supplementary psychotherapeutic treatment, it becomes evident that the supposedly "endogenic illness" is produced in fact principally through the nature of the family conflict. Out of her unconscious rivalry, the woman provokes her husband's depression (he thereupon enters into the role of her "weak part") in order to escape the threatening danger of self-hatred. For she herself has become possessed by the phallic-narcissistic desire to dominate, which she once admired in him but which she has long since incorporated into herself. Because secretly she is terrified that she may lose her acquired overcompensatory masculinity, she is unable to yield to her husband so much as a handbreadth of the power position in the family. Unconsciously she feels that her structure of overcompensation would collapse like a house of cards.

From this basis, her conflict drives her again and again to a deadly game with her husband: his periodic breakdowns are designed to protect her from the decompensation which she believes she must inevitably fall victim to in case of a renewed subjection to her husband. An anxiety that is understandable, given her psychic make-up.

Impotence and Frigidity in Alternation

Another example: A man who has been disguising his self-doubt through overcompensation marries a frigid woman. To begin with, she represents for him his "negative identity," she stands for the weakness that he refuses at any price to admit in himself. And her failure to experience sexual sensation conveys to him a feeling of unchallenged manly strength, which he self-deceptively attributes to himself. The sexually disturbed woman helps him to conceal how passive and uncertain of his own potency he secretly is. So he has especially chosen this frigid partner because he would be afraid of failure with a woman who was fully responsive sexually. When in the course of the marriage she more and more frequently denies her husband's sexual wishes because she finds coitus unpleasant, conflicts arise. And so one day the wife goes into psychotherapy.

In case after case, frigidity can be effectively treated psychotherapeutically. Thus it comes about that the young wife in the course of psychotherapy not only learns to experience sexual desire but achieves orgasm as well. And, as not infrequent in such cases, her sexual need, so long neurotically repressed, increases rapidly. She desires frequent sexual contact—and now discovers to her astonishment that her husband evades her and on occasion is even impotent. The fact that the wife is no longer a small, weak, disappointing person but in point of sexual capacity his equal—indeed, threatens to exceed him—is not easily bearable. This indicates that in accord with his psychic make-up he regards sexual contact as narcissistic competition rather than loving communion. The important thing in his eyes is less the giving and receiving of pleasure than victory or defeat.

And now the fear of defeat is real. The more pressing this fear becomes, the more unendurable the disgrace of occasionally not satisfying his wife sexually. In order to avoid these situations, he extends the interval between sexual contact more and more, just as his wife had originally done.

There are many marriages in which for years this sort of rivalry-conflict rages. It is just one of the partners who is truly potent or capable of orgasm, as the case may be; the other functions badly or at times fails completely. This too is a typical group neurosis, sustained through an interaction conflict. To be exact, it is a symptom neurosis with a more or less cyclical transference of symptoms. The overt sexual disturbance of the one partner is, if you like, only the expression of the marriage neurosis. The apparently healthy partner is actually involved to the same degree in the occurrence of the illness as the symptom bearer himself.

The Child Grows Up, the Mother Falls Ill

Another type of family neurosis involves overprotective mothers. Here it can happen either that the mother drives the child into developing symptoms or the other way around; if the child succeeds in emancipating itself, the mother is driven into symptom formation.

The overprotective mother, as is well known, tends to make her child anxious and lacking in self-confidence, in order to keep it in symbiotic dependence.[58] Often, an overprotected and restricted child comes to play the role of partner substitute. The mother, to be sure, conducts herself in a domineering and oppressive manner, even though she herself is in an infantile, passive way dependent upon the child's not leaving her and supplying her constantly with evidences of affection. Frequently, a mother of this sort suffers from some deep disturbance for which she partially compensates by clinging to her child. The child gives her a sense of stability because it is compelled to acknowledge her importance constantly through expressions of love and gratitude. If the child falls ill with an anxiety neurosis, loss of social contact, disturbance in eating or sleeping, the mother readily accepts it. The neurosis stabilizes the child's dependency, and the mother now feels less concerned that the neurotically weakened child may break away from the symbiosis. However, as soon as the growing child is able to protect itself more effectively against her domination, the mother falls at once into a depressed state. In this phase there is frequently an escalation of childish outbursts of defiance in response to despairing maternal complaints. With a flood of accusations and threats, the mother continues to try to deprive her child of the strength to break free and realize itself. She fears her imminent isolation like death, foreseeing that she will react to it with a depression. In her increasing anxiety, she develops various disturbances of the sympathetic nervous system: palpitations of the heart, chest pains, headaches, nausea. Fresh arguments to crush the child, if possible, with even greater feelings of guilt. These symptoms are, of course, only an expression of the mother's personal fears and are wholly unjustified instruments of blackmail. But in her increasing desperation the mother becomes blind to the choice of means used to reach her single goal: to hold the child firmly in the old symbiosis.

Often enough, this disastrous strategy finally leads once more to "success." The child, driven into a corner, capitulates; the mother recovers and honors the "insight" of the defeated child by occasional indulgences. In the history of such neurotic situations, there develops as a rule a family character alteration of the anxiety-neurotic type (see chapter 6).

If, however, the mother fails in her efforts and the child wins out against all her attempts to undermine it, she usually suffers a severe breakdown. She must now inescapably take upon herself the consequences of her unresolved conflict, which she had formerly imposed upon her child. In this sense, we have here, too, "a social transference of symptoms": like that in the case of alternating sexual neurosis described above.

The phenomenon of symptom transference in family neuroses should be given much more attention in medicine. These typical case histories and those to follow may serve to show that it is a commonplace occurrence. Medicine has not hitherto paid special attention to this phenomenon, because it does not fit into the concept of individual treatment. On the contrary, taking it into account systematically would affect many statistics denoting therapeutic success. The proportion of success in single treatment in psychological medicine is naturally more impressive if one uses as the criterion individual symptom improvement. In that case, nothing is said about the apparent successes that consist in the medical improvement of a single patient while his place is taken by a new symptom bearer, who from then on must serve as safety valve for the unimproved group tension.

In the future, research in psychosomatic therapy will not be able to limit itself to the investigation of the individual if its statistics are to carry conviction. Those patients who instead of gaining a genuine cure through therapy simply learn to channel the pressure of their inner conflicts through social partners and at their expense can no longer naïvely be counted on the success side of the ledger. One can no longer simply ask:

What has happened to the individual who had psychotherapy? One must ask at the same time: What is happening to the persons in the family closest to the patient? Only then can the true psychotherapeutic successes be brought out. These, to be specific, are the cases in which an analyzed individual through his increased inner freedom learns to exert a positive influence on the group of which he is a part.

TYPES OF FAMILY CHARACTER NEUROSES

6

The Anxiety-Neurotic Family
CATCHWORD: SANITARIUM

Family symptom neuroses cannot be systematically divided. Certain categories are useful but do not provide precise references. One could, for example, differentiate between families which only periodically provide themselves with a safety valve for their tensions through a symptom bearer and those families which require a permanent means of release for their conflicts via a symptom bearer. One might further classify symptom-neurotic families according to whether they rotate symptom transference among themselves or stick to a permanent division of the family—the ever "healthy" or the ever "sick." These formal distinctions, however, are not basic enough to justify detailed investigation. There is much more to be gained from the systematic classification of family character neuroses. One of their chief features consists in just this, that the families in question organize themselves with relative unanimity according to a consistent neurotic concept which can always be described as such and can be differentiated qualitatively from other concepts.

Character-neurotic families always show one of a small number of leitmotivs which color everything they do. If one tries to sum up the leitmotivs in a single word, there are, for example, *sanitarium* (for families suffering from anxiety neurosis), *theater* (for hysterical families), or *fortress* (for paranoid families).

The character-neurotic family adapts its whole life to a common theme—or, more accurately, limits its life to that. The specifically neurotic factor is the narrowness of the theme; also, the rigid compulsion to follow only that. There is no improvisation, no play, no experimentation with new leitmotivs. Every child must fit from the beginning into the one rigid, thematic concept. He can pick out for himself only a role that fits precisely into the dramatic script. Any deviation from this prepared role threatens the laboriously erected defense system of the family, breaches the specific bulwark set up against fear and desperation. As a result, this family would be endangered by any outsider, for in contrast to the symptom-neurotic family it bases its defense not on intrafamily divisions and rejection procedures but on intrafamily solidarity. A mutual overidentification takes place. The acting out of the conflict occurs jointly and outwardly. Confrontation with intrafamily tensions is avoided by a denial of the internal group problem, which is pushed outside the family. In such cases, therefore, the processes of splitting up and isolation do not take place between one part of the family and another but between the family collectively and the outside world. And certain types of character-neurotic families can be described on the basis of the specific concealments, avoidances, or ideological structures by means of which they create a private world, which helps them to evade the genuine obligations of social reality.

To be sure, the solidarity of a character-neurotic family can under certain circumstances collapse. When an activating member drops out, the collective defense system may become unstable without him. Or when a child of the family who has grown up objects stoutly to the prescribed role which is supposed to fit him into the collective neurotic system, processes of disintegration may set in, and the character-neurotic configuration may be transformed into a symptom-neurotic constellation. Examples of this will be given in the chapters on -paranoid and hysterical families.

In anxiety-neurotic families, it is characteristic that the family "group ego" shrinks under the influence of terrifying fears. The family creates for itself a sanitarium-like protective world which it attempts by every possible means to guard against anxiety-causing stimuli. The following typical example describes such a change in a family's character—and the results.

A member of the family fell ill with a cardiac-neurosis (anxiety neurosis) phobia. The attacks of panic or, as it may have been, of phobic dread regularly increased the patient's need to cling to the member of the family closest to him. As has been fully described elsewhere,[79] the cardiac-neurotic promises himself magical protection from his fears through symbiotic clinging to the person closest to him. Like little children who can play fearlessly only in the presence of their mothers, he irrationally attributes to the presence of his associate a protective power against the danger of an attack of panic. Many of these patients, out of fear of separation, are barely able to undertake anything at all by themselves. They must have their relatives around them constantly. And they are afraid not simply of situations of isolation but of any event that carries the possibilities of a mishap. For they are full of imperfectly suppressed expectations of doom. And so, pedantically quoting maxims, they tend to avoid every kind of undertaking in which they or their relatives might suffer injury. More than that, many of these cardiac neurotics, or phobic patients, cannot stand conversations, books, or films in which any disaster is portrayed, which in their pessimistic timidity they picture as befalling them. They cannot even look at a crime or suspense movie on television without feeling panic. In the newspapers they skip, so far as possible, reports of accidents, natural catastrophes, crimes of violence, accounts of wars, and the like. And by preference they leave the room if the family table talk or social conversation turns on sickness, death, automobile accidents, or other unhappy events. These people have to indulge in the illusion that around them there is only peace, harmony, health, and a safeguarded life. They use their notion of a safe, sheltered world like a wrapping to protect their highly vulnerable psychic equilibrium from dangerous agitations. They have to make enormous efforts to hold down the pessimistic dread that constantly threatens to overwhelm their ego. All their foresight and renunciation is intended to hold in check like a great dam the latent fear of annihilation, which in the acute phases of the illness takes the form of volcanic disorders of the sympathetic nervous system.

Now, with a new cardiac patient, one frequently sees the relatives at first trying to defend themselves against the patient's intensive tendency to cling. They rebel first of all against the patient's wish to limit various common undertakings through all possible precautionary, safety measures. They are not satisfied with watching only light and harmless programs on television. And they do not like to be told that they can talk about nothing but agreeable, gratifying things at the table. In short, they rebel against having their freedom of action reduced by the sick member of the family. But with the passage of time they are worn down by the insistence of the patient. His reproach that they are ruthlessly disregarding his health leads to feelings of guilt and makes them acquiescent. And so finally they form, together with the sick person, a symbiotic ocnophile* group. They stick together as much as possible and collectively avoid confrontation with exciting, disquieting problems. In the interests of the sick person, the family reconstitutes itself as a kind of sanitarium. And in fact the patient often reacts with corresponding improvement of his symptoms after he has succeeded in having the immediate causes of his attacks of panic radically reduced.

The psychoanalyst recognizes that the individual illness of the patient has thereby been masked, that the whole family is now acting out his phobia, withdrawing into the soothing atmosphere of a sanitarium world. To see or hear nothing more about wickedness, about cruelty, injustice, danger—in accordance with this motto, a kind of eventless *vita minima* is established. A definite type of collective curtailment of the ego takes

---

* Ocnophilia is a concept introduced into psychoanalysis by M. Balint. It designates a particular fear of risks and is associated with a need for close association.

place. Through phobic reaction formation and avoidance, there follows a retreat of the family into an insular, narcissistic form of existence in which, as in an actual sanitarium, only that portion of agreeable impressions and unexciting events is admitted that will pass through the filter of hygienic standards. Through this artificial narrowing of their lives, the family maneuvers itself far from the stream of the important impulses and strong emotions of daily life into an intellectual isolation which, to be sure, is hardly felt as painful—especially by the patient—since it is compensated for by the more highly valued freedom from excitement.

And so sometimes the manifest neurotic illness of the original patient disappears—or, to be more accurate, becomes latent. The soothing climate of the altered family atmosphere has reversed the affected individual's sickness and reduced it to a symptomless, quiescent stage. But, obviously, the family has paid a high price for this. It has exchanged the medical problem of a single person for the collective ego contraction or ego impoverishment of the whole group. The result is a partial dulling and immobilization—that is, a serious sacrifice in social effectiveness.

This example shows once more the unsatisfactory one-sidedness of the traditional concept of health when applied uncritically in psychological medicine. This way of compensating for an individual neurosis within the family at the expense of collective loss of freedom cannot with good conscience be declared a cure. Indeed, one would be quite right in raising the question whether phobic ego contraction of the whole family under the pressure of the sick individual has not increased the damage rather than reduced it. The egosyntonic phobia now acted out by the whole group is in certain respects far more dangerous than the original individual illness that has been concealed by it. Once the family has ceased to suffer from the sacrifice involved in its own reduced freedom of action and begins to assimilate its new sanitarium-like style as an obligatory standard, it is well on the way to irreparable psychosocial deformation.

And it is hardly surprising that the children in such families generally grow up to be highly timorous, hypochondriac persons subject to attacks of cardiac neurosis.[79] As the phobic alteration in the family's character becomes more and more firmly rooted, the danger increases that the defect will become a fixed tradition over several generations.

Nevertheless, in many families which have compensated for the cardiac neurosis or the phobia of one of its members, there often remains for a long time some consciousness of the unnaturalness of the sacrifice they are making for the sick person. This becomes evident, for example, when those concerned are questioned later. If inquiry is made about how things stand with the cardiac neurotics or the phobics several years after the first investigations, it often happens that the replies of the patients differ from those of the family (Ernst,[25] Beckmann, Richter, and Scheer[5]). Sometimes a patient will assert that he is cured, whereas the members of his family, on the contrary, say his anxieties are as bad as ever. The contradiction is easy to explain.

The patient feels he is cured as soon as his considerate, thoughtful relatives spare him most of the former causes of alarm. He has comfortably adapted himself to the sanitarium atmosphere which has become to him a matter of course. The relatives, however, are aware of the continued existence of his illness as long as they are aware of the self-sacrifice they were compelled to make in order to create the unnatural climate of consideration demanded by the patient. Not until this tension-arousing feeling in the relatives has disappeared and they have come to terms painlessly with their restricted sphere of activity will they deem that the sick man is well. Then the regressive change in the family character is complete. All now regard the new hospital-like life style of the family as normal. The following case contains many, though not all, of the major characteristics just described in the sketch of an anxiety-neurotic family.

Three Little Rabbits in a Trap

A vigorous master workman who behaves like a patriarch and his timid, conventional wife have a daughter. Vital and enterprising in herself, the girl becomes highly uneasy in the company of men who seek her acquaintance. A strong unconscious tie to her father, guilt feelings due to rivalry with her ailing mother, and traces of the mother's narrow-minded moral code inhibit the girl from accepting romantic attachments. Observers are amazed at this timidity, which is in such obvious contrast to the girl's ardent thirst for activity. A few times she encounters impetuous and fiery suitors, but always recoils in a sudden access of fear when the relationship threatens to become more intimate. Finally she marries the exact opposite of the acquaintances she has hitherto preferred: a quite unimpressive, anxiously prudent civil servant. The husband is highly competent and well thought of in his department. But his compulsive pedantry and caution keep him from gaining the recognition due his professional gifts and keep him from cutting an impressive figure. The case is perfectly clear: the uncertain young woman has chosen this reliable, safe partner as a refuge because the more colorful, imposing acquaintances of past years inspired her with too much fear. With her husband she believes she is absolutely secure: he is a model of fidelity, thoughtfulness, and propriety. Also, despite his ascetic traits, he is quite tolerant and allows her freedom of action. She can pursue her hobbies unhindered, cultivate what friends she likes, buy furniture, clothes, and so forth, to her heart's content. It never occurs to her to abuse his generosity, but she has nevertheless a satisfying feeling of freedom in these areas.

And yet she repeatedly and unexpectedly encounters momentary temptations. The husband of one of her friends and later one of her husband's superiors begins to woo her. At a party he finally presses her with unmistakable intent. She feels his physical excitement while dancing. He arranges a weekend party at his country house, in which several families take part, and contrives an opportunity to see the woman alone, and this time he attacks her sexually. She is greatly upset and although she continues to defend herself is nevertheless unable to make a definite break with him.

During the following nights she cannot sleep and a week later comes down with a typical cardiac-neurotic anxiety attack. For several hours she experiences wild heart palpitations. She becomes dizzy. It seems to her that she cannot get her breath, every moment she expects her heart to stop. Later it will become evident that this attack and her persisting excessive anxiety are results of the unresolved temptation conflict. Almost at the point of giving herself to her fascinating acquaintance, she falls into a state of panic because the impulse to disloyalty threatens to upset the self-confidence she has laboriously built up through the symbiotic arrangement with her husband. The sequel: a further retreat into childlike, correct, compulsive conduct. For weeks she remains under medical treatment, fears serious heart trouble, and is admittedly depressed. Then she slowly recovers. But she thenceforth avoids her dangerous acquaintance and in general limits her social activities. The unexpected death of her mother from a heart attack is a further blow, to which she is obviously not able to adjust. More easily than before, she loses her emotional balance, weeps a great deal, and remains concerned about the state of her heart although no doctor can find anything wrong with it.

From this time on, she clings more closely to her husband. He is happy to meet these needs. Often disquieted before by his wife's impulsive temperament, he willingly acquiesces in her desire to cut off contacts for both of them outside the family, and inside the family to concentrate entirely on peace, thoughtfulness, prudence, hygiene, and denial of conflict. Meanwhile, the little daughter born to the couple is completely drawn into this hospital atmosphere of consideration. Husband and wife develop the habit of addressing each other as "Mama" and "Papa"—one of the many signs of regressive infantilization of the whole family constellation. Anxiety, feelings of faintness, and hundreds of prophylactic measures against imagined accidents characterize the home situation. Husband and wife behave toward each other like children who are brother and sister. They play the roles of mature married people and parents somewhat in the manner of a superficial "as if." They act out the appropriate characteristics of their roles without being able to fill them with their own identities. When they call each other Mama and Papa, it means that they are seeing themselves to a certain extent with the eyes of a child—or, to be more exact, with their own childhood eyes.

Since this reciprocal clinging together, in which the child

is of course involved, is not enough to assuage the parents' *angst,* they have recourse to another defense mechanism already briefly mentioned: they treat the rules of bourgeois morality and hygiene as "phantom parents." Just as timid children meticulously obey the orders of their parents so as not to lose their protection, they are at pains to follow to the letter various cautionary rules; they go to bed punctually at an early hour, eat lightly and according to a dietetic plan, are painstakingly moderate in their drinking. They do not read much, in order to spare their eyes. The television is turned off early, so it will not interfere with their going to sleep. They avoid any company that might excite them too much or be too strenuous or in some other way unwholesome. Sexual intercourse is hygienically scheduled: Saturday evening, if it is not too late, or Sunday morning—so that they can be sure of proper rest afterward. If it should ever happen accidentally on a weekday —inadvertently, perhaps a glass too much of wine was to blame —their conscience smites them at once: they really shouldn't have done it. Next time they will have to be more careful.

They keep withdrawing from acquaintances and events that might disturb their tranquillity. They pay with a good conscience for healthy food, solid household furnishings—and make cautious investments, content with low dividends. Naturally they read a bourgeois, conservative newspaper that stands for compromise, order, and safety and presents any disturbing events of the day in so muted a manner that the shock to the nerves is cushioned and harmless. If politics actually becomes a threat, they would prefer a half truth and untroubled sleep at night to confrontation with the whole truth and the risk of losing their equilibrium.

"Small am I and pure of heart!" This is the motto expressing an attitude of complete humility with which they unconsciously hope to avoid the vengeance of the envious gods (in their own superegos). This is why they no longer venture anything original, outstanding, or daring in any sphere of life. They dress as conventionally and correctly as possible, furnish their home modestly, and drive an inconspicuous make of car. Of course they support a conservative morality and are dumfounded at the fiery protests of the young. Thus, both husband and wife retreat, so to speak, into a sheltered, peaceful refuge which they believe they have made impregnable with the bunker walls of their system of disavowal. And the servile observation of the moral and hygienic tables of the law are, as we have said, nothing but phantom parents created by projection (or from early memories, as the case may be) who seem to promise security and well-being as rewards for strict obedience.

Whereas for the husband this life style is really only a logical extension of his old compulsive, neurotic contraction of the ego, the woman's fate marks a striking change. And yet it was she who, after the eruption of her anxiety attacks, domineeringly imposed upon the family the creation of a hospital atmosphere. Of her former natural impulsiveness hardly anything remains. Within a few months this fresh, vital person has become transformed into an elderly invalid constantly afraid that through one false step or some small frivolity she will conjure up horrible catastrophes. She must continue—so the psychoanalytical interpretation would read—to play the role of anxious, ailing mother as punishment for her Oedipal sexual desires through which she believes unconsciously she was guilty of her mother's death.

It follows as a matter of course that the little daughter must join in the hospital game. She is led by the hand longer, she is warned more emphatically about every danger and evil than other children are. The basic feeling communicated to her, unconsciously to be sure, and yet almost intentionally, is uncertainty and the anxious anticipation of misfortune. "Just be sure that nothing happens to you!" is the mother's most frequent advice to her daughter. Only in this way, she believes, can the child develop the alertness necessary to avoid in time the dangers of illness, accident, seduction, and so forth. The selfish neurotic motive of keeping the child always at her disposal, as an object to cling to and always do her will, remains hidden from her consciousness.

The little one is soon overtaxed: always to be clean, quiet, modest, totally unaggressive, always attentive, self-controlled— all this exceeds her powers. Soon she begins to show the early symptoms of an anxiety neurosis. Her parents appear not at all disturbed by this. Just as they have come to regard their own timorous ego-shrinking not as a sickness but rather as especially intelligent foresight, a reasonable adaptation to the dangers of the world, so they rejoice that "our child knows how to look out for herself!" The beginning of what may be perhaps a life-long infantile neurosis they greet as the first stage in a successful cautionary education. In any case, they know now that their child will necessarily fit into the family "sanitarium" created by them and that she will willingly participate in the artificial sterility of their anxiety-neurotic life style.

Just as there was a statistically provable increase in the number of cardiac neuroses after World War II (Jorswieck and Katwan,[56] Christian,[16] Richter and Beckmann[79]), so clinical impressions also indicate an increase in family constellations suffering from anxiety neuroses. The disturbingly high quota of family structures deformed by anxiety neuroses is to be evaluated by no means simply or even primarily as a purely clinical problem but first as a problem of special sociological significance. The indicated dynamic of anxiety neurosis, even when the change in the family's character is not very pronounced, always involves a growing rigidity of the partnership bonds within the family, accompanied by the characteristics of an immature symbiosis. Those involved cling to each other in order to gain joint protection against the imagined threat of dangers from every direction—and naturally forfeit in this defensive attitude the possibilities of free, progressive development. This type of family neurosis often has in addition an ideological superstructure: the phobic need of clinging together or the inability to leave a protective partner without chaotic outbursts of anxiety is reinterpreted as a freely chosen attitude of constancy and superior propriety. Members of anxiety-neurotic families react with expressions of horror to examples of freer sexual attitudes, extramarital sexual relationships, divorces, and so forth in their circle and are often simply compensating with this reaction formation for the danger of devastating envy of the fearlessness and openness to life with which healthier people form their partnerships.

In fact, the life of the anxiety-neurotic family shows outwardly all the signs of bourgeois decorum, to the point of complete idyllic harmony. Exemplary in its reliability appears the bond between husband and wife, and the continued close relationship of the children to their parents even after the age of maturity may awaken the envy of many whose children opposed them at an early age and insisted on going their own ways. "Thank God we don't have those problems with our children!" one hears not infrequently from parents exhibiting signs of anxiety neurosis but proudly pointing to the treasured principles of conservative educational ethics.

In reality, however, anxiety is the principal motive for the pseudo-harmonious clustering together of the anxiety-neurotic families. They could not get away from one another even if they wanted to, because not one of them can exist alone by himself without experiencing a complete collapse of self-confidence. If the dangers to marriage typical of these times and the worldwide problems of the new generation in gaining independence are in general fewer or at least milder in anxiety-neurotic families, the principal reason for this is that these people have not yet achieved the stage of maturity at which such problems first become acute. They sit chattering together in their self-created hospital world, inhibited children all of them—and no one risks the clear and open expression of his differences with his family partners.

Research in our psychosomatic clinic at the University of Giessen has produced interesting evidence of this. Over a period of five years we have examined more than a hundred and fifty cardiac-neurotic (anxiety-neurotic) adults with typical attacks and phobic symptoms and have also studied their family relationships in detail.[79] Complete or partially realized anxiety-neurotic family structures were found in a majority of cases. As expected, the proportion of single or divorced patients was significantly smaller than for the average population in this age group, and also smaller than in a control group of other neurotics. And so it is not only individual observations but exact statistical data as well that point quite clearly to the greater inclination toward symbiosis of anxiety neurotics, proved by the relative frequency of their marriages. In our analysis of the family structure, it often turned out that the marriage partners had little respect for each other or even hated each other bitterly.

Many believed they were not at all suitable marriage partners and only tormented each other. Hostile confusions and impulsive bickering were common in the everyday life of these families. But almost always there was something theatrical and impermanent about the quarrels, like the behavior of nervous children who know from the start that they have to put up with one another because they could not stand a really serious, even if brief, isolation from each other. We saw many anxiety-neurotic members of such families who in month-long therapy poured out a flood of complaints about their marriage partners, without being capable of even the thought of enduring the consequences of a definitive showdown. Even more abjectly than the adults, the children in anxiety-neurotic families naturally remain in symbiotic dependency, incapable of finding a truly independent road for themselves or of ever asserting their claims against their parents. One sees sons and daughters over forty sitting at table in their parents' homes as timid and abashed as they were thirty years before, or bringing their own families into their parents' houses as hesitantly as schoolchildren who timidly beg their parents to recognize the schoolmates they have brought home with them.

Although, according to recent medical statistics, more men than women consult doctors because of anxiety-neurotic (cardiac-neurotic) difficulties, obviously women more often precipitate marked anxiety-neurotic changes in the family than do men. This corresponds, too, with the findings of a representative survey (carried out under the direction of our clinic at the Divo Institute in Frankfurt), according to which middle-aged or older women in West Germany report on the average a great many more anxieties than men of all ages and young women.[6]

Those answering the questionnaire were asked to check a number on a seven-point scale ranging from "I consider myself very seldom anxious" to "I consider myself unusually anxious":

$$3 \; 2 \; 1 \; 0 \; 1 \; 2 \; 3$$

The zero was to be marked if the person considered herself exactly as much or as little anxious as the average.

In their answers, the women in the age group between thirty-five and sixty differed from the men of the same age or less by one full point to the right—that is, in the direction of "unusually anxious." The younger women graded themselves as less anxious in comparison with them, but still definitely more anxious than the men.

The answers to another statement were similar: "I believe I am comparatively unworried about other people | (3 2 1 0 1 2 3) | very much worried about other people."

Here, too, middle-aged and older women showed a more definite deviation to the right (and greater worry) in their answers, than all other groups.

We are dealing here not with the occasional observations of limited medical practice or a single clinic but with a representative sample of the citizens of the West German Republic. And so if the women in this country, at an age at which as house-wives and mothers they have maximum influence in their families, express on the average pronounced anxiety and feel very worried about other people, it follows that among them there must be a considerable proportion of out-and-out anxiety neurotics involved in serious intrafamily reactions. Unquestionably, then, the anxiety-neurotic family dynamic just described is not by any means an extreme phenomenon chosen from among the curiosities in the psychotherapist's collection but a mass phenomenon of particular social significance.

Whatever changes are brought about in the structure of traditional family life—say, in the direction of communal living, or freer behavior in the partner relationships, etc.—will be regarded as evil by the numerous families distorted by anxiety neurosis and contraction of the ego. They will consider as a threat every experiment and every development in the direction of a greater opening of the family inwardly or outwardly, and will try to put a stop to it. These families must necessarily condemn every loosening of the close-knit, tightly cemented relationships established through inherited taboos and restrictive standards, although there can be no question that that part of society now attaining voting age will be able to develop the forms and limits of modern family life only on the basis of freer, personal decisions, no longer by submitting to the dictates of the law.

After all these critical observations concerning the unfavorable aspects of the anxiety-neurotic family configuration and its influences on society, an explanatory note must be added. It holds as well for the other forms of family character distortion to be described in the following chapters. Medical and especially psychiatric concepts of what is normal impinge more and more on traditional moral standards. Neurotic, psychopathic, psychotic ("crazy")—these are generally considered more damning epithets than "bad" or "evil." It is therefore most confusing for uninitiated readers of psychoanalytical writings to read descriptions of some of their own character traits, since they would detest being regarded as abnormal by psychiatrists or psychoanalysts.

Now in every family there are traces of anxiety-neurotic, hysterical, or paranoid structural characteristics, and one must remember that psychoanalysis does not have a different vocabulary for the normal from the one used for the psychically aberrant and pathological. For this reason, psychoanalysts even in their diagnostic descriptions of people who correspond approximately to the standard norm make use of degrees of hysteria, anxiety-neurosis, paranoia, depression, and so forth, as convenient terms to characterize the personality structure. This lack of a clear verbal differentiation in turn is possible only because, as already noted, we all exhibit traits of one or another form of neurosis, usually indeed of several in some special combination. Nietzsche, and after him, in a more differentiated and precise form, Freud and his followers revealed how much childishness, unperceived irrational fantasy and impulse motivate the behavior of even the so-called normal adult. We should feel ashamed of this discovery and strive to eliminate the irrational determinants of our behavior, instead of reacting with a neurotic defense by denying the painful truth and making Freud the scapegoat—as though, instead of unmasking the neurotic load we all carry, Freud had invented it!

The frequently heard accusation that psychoanalysts are maliciously inclined to find something neurotic in everyone springs from just this attempt to transform the discovery of a painful reality into a vicious fiction. And so psychoanalysis is assailed because it is steadfastly trying to destroy one of the most stubborn and vain illusions of mankind. The illusion is that as a matter of course society consists exclusively of self-aware beings governed by reason and able at any time to examine fearlessly their intentions and impulses—something which, as we know today, is possible only after prolonged psychoanalysis, and then to a limited degree.

This makes it all the more a social obligation to recognize and control the influences of infantile, irrational, emotional impulses in our behavior, the extent of which is only slowly becoming evident. The realization of this necessity is what makes the confrontation with our present unsatisfactory state so terrifying but so indispensable. Among other things, we must understand, for example, that many traditional moral concepts and assertions of our rights (especially family rights) are nothing but collective reaction formations based on immature fears. To the degree to which we are able to overcome, in particular, the anxiety-neurotic elements in the determinants of our family structures, we will be able to discover which freely chosen forms of family life we can retain in society, or some day develop anew.

7

The Paranoid Family
CATCHWORD: FORTRESS

While the anxiety-neurotic family principally narrows its view
of reality by resorting to a variety of fear-conditional concealments and avoidances, the paranoid family transforms reality
through illusionary notions. It must be said at once that the
words "paranoid" and "illusionary" are not meant in the
narrower psychiatric sense. Only in extreme cases does a
family suffering from a paranoid character disturbance con-
struct a true clinical system of illusion. Much more often, these
families systematically overvalue only certain protective ideas
or ideologies, behind which they mobilize and desperately defend
themselves. Between the anxiety-neurotic type of family and the
paranoid type, transitions are easy. The anxiety-neurotic family
is living, literally, not only in a limited reality but in one that
has been qualitatively changed in content. By carefully hiding
from their area of perception the elements of aggression,
violence, and death, they make for themselves a shrunken and
qualitatively altered "remnant of a world." This, if one likes,
could be regarded as the beginning of an illusory reconstruc-
tion of reality. The truly paranoid family changes the world
not only by means of phobic denials and evasions but at the
same time through active, systematic reinterpretation. It con-

structively rethinks reality—and thereby manages to remove the contradiction between its concept of reality and its concept of itself. Paranoia offers many families their last chance for solidarity, which ordinarily, because of the unusual pressure of unmastered aggression, could not be attained in any other way.

One often finds among paranoid families a couple or a larger group who again and again successfully manage to discharge unbearable, reciprocal, hostile impulses outwardly against individuals, groups, or philosophies of life. They create for themselves the fiction of getting along well together by externalizing their internal group problem and seeking in the world about them targets for reproaches that are really aimed at each other and originally, mostly unconsciously, against their own egos.

Usually, one member of a marriage functions as the nucleus for crystallizing the system of illusion. Most often, this is the more active, irritable, fanatical member. Once he (or she) has taken up a paranoid position, there is a great pressure on the marriage partner and the other members of the family either to join him (or her) or to adopt a polarized, hostile position themselves. The friend-or-foe way of hallucinatory thinking really leaves only the choice between comradeship-in-arms or constant, uncompromising enmity. And so it is easy to understand that overawed members of the family often become slavish followers, even when initially they found it very hard to understand the distorted life view of their relative. No doubt it is the uncanny, penetrating power radiating from a paranoid personality that triumphs over all intellectual criticism. This is the only way one can explain the occasional epidemic spread of abnormal, overvalued ideas in times of sharp group polarization. Anyone who does not have a firmly established personal identity is apparently, in certain circumstances, even against his better judgment, open to the suggestive attraction of a paranoid system of thought that promises instantaneous discharge of all threatening intra-individual or intragroup tensions.

Dupont and Grunebaum[21] have recently published an illuminating study of the marriage structure of nine hallucinating women (not schizophrenics). In all nine cases, the husbands took a more or less active part in the illusionary behavior of their wives. In particular, the following remarkable correlations were found:

The women had chosen as husbands men who were rather passive, socially isolated, and inhibited sexually. In general, these men were unable to assert themselves professionally in positions of responsibility. As a rule, the wives had been subject to paranoic illness at one time, during which their husbands had increasingly withdrawn from them. During this phase, sexual relations usually ceased. The men proved unable to protect themselves against the bizarre, unnatural behavior of their wives. As "willing sacrifices," they not only allowed themselves to be drawn into the hallucinations but, by cooperating with their wives, contributed to the worsening of the illness.

If, in the end, confinement of the patients in a clinic was necessary, it came about not as a decision of the husbands, or even with their consent, but always through intervention from outside. The husbands, indeed, rebelled along with their wives against confinement in a clinic and the necessary temporary separation, being absolutely unaware of the wives' need of treatment.

In this instance, to be sure, a true delusional illness is present; that is, more than a simple change of character in the sense of a family character neurosis. But even here it is notable that the two people are unable to realize the pathological seriousness of the overt disturbance. Within the family, all consciousness of illness is missing. Only an incident involving outside society will show the situation is a "medical case"—to this extent, one can classify it as an extreme variant in the category of family character disturbances.

Through paranoia the couple compensate for their formerly almost hopelessly disturbed marriage. This is a case of literal *folie à deux* by which a severely distorted marriage relationship threatened with collapse is temporarily bolstered. Quite logically, Dupont and Grunebaum consider it inadequate to explain this illusion formation simply as a problem in the individual psychopathology of women. Ultimately, like the anxiety-neurotic type of family ego-disturbance described above, these disturbances are based on a common dialogic conflict between the partners.

Now, of course, in most cases of family paranoid disturbances, as we have said, there is no hallucination in the narrower psychiatric sense. It is simply a case of families controlled by unusually marked, one-sided, overvalued ideas. Characteristically, these ideas are held with a fierce, fanatical tenacity, and usually they become systematized into an ideology.

Some examples may clarify the essentials of the paranoid family structure. The first, rich in dramatic touches, shows a gradual transition from a hysterical to a paranoid family dynamic.

We'll Show Them!

A successful merchant of very modest Silesian origins marries a girl fifteen years younger than he. Outwardly, no greater contrast could be conceived than that of the squat, middle-aged man with bad eyes and the slim, beautiful woman who, only after prolonged and stubborn resistance, surrenders to his equally persistent wooing. But it is just this mutual stubbornness at the onset of a decades-long marriage drama that shows the two to be as similar in psychic structure as they are different in outward appearance. Both can be unyielding to the point of fanaticism—the outwardly so delicate-looking young woman to an even greater degree than her husband. And each feels in the other the same ambition and will to power. She, still rather childish and inexperienced, feels attracted by his brilliant professional success and by his worldly life style and is determined with his help to rid herself of the mortifying poverty she grew up in. For him she serves as an ornament—elflike, delicate, and admired on all sides—and as a compensation, too, for his unattractive, coarse appearance; and he hopes above all for an even more important position, aided by her determination to succeed. On both sides, it is a predominantly "narcissistic" choice of partners. Each supplies the other with exactly the instrument that was hitherto missing for the fulfillment of his own high-flown ambitions. Dependency needs on the part of the husband, which will become very evident later in the marriage, do not at first appear as an important motive.

Almost in a spirit of intoxication, they share the belief that together they can work wonders. The dominant theme of the new marriage is a dream of power and grandeur which in the beginning seems only harmless exuberance but by degrees takes on more and more fanatical traits. It is an insidiously developing rivalry between husband and wife that adds fuel to this ambitious fanaticism. The young wife proves not to be the type of self-effacing helper who delegates a part of her ambition to her husband and through participation in his successes is able to find satisfaction for herself. Despite her almost childlike appearance and the substantial difference in their ages, she disputes from the beginning his leading role in the marriage and defends every inch of ground. The dreams of grandeur developed together and fought for with ever-increasing stubbornness then prove a temporary refuge from the danger of mutual destruction.

They build a house designed like a castle—naturally, the most stately dwelling for miles around; they have children, more and finer, they believe, than anyone else's. The five children are given fantastically strange first names. Each time the registrar protests, not wishing to enter such names. But—as in everything else—the husband and wife have their way. Just as unique and incomparable as they feel they are, so must their children be too—and with names to match.

Not all five, to be sure, turn out to be the expected model children. With almost barbaric sternness, they are compelled to present strong, superior personalities in the outside world but within the family must become objects of manipulation, practically without a will of their own. One daughter is troublesome, a little difficult, a little defiant. Blows rain upon her. Finally a strict boarding school is chosen to break her will and prepare her for docile submission to her parents' regime.

Even after the birth of five children—within seven years—the wife has not given up any part of her lofty, egocentric pretensions. She embarks on various flirtations. Her attempts to lure interesting men into her clutches are impelled by an insatiable will to power. She carries on these conquests before the eyes of her gradually aging husband. The husband avenges himself by beating her. She endures his maltreatment unbowed.

The marriage battle for power at times assumes grotesque forms. At one moment it looks as though the vulnerable, easily angered man will one day be moved to excessive brutality, so cynical are the provocations to which his wife in her rivalry constantly subjects him. But something different and unexpected happens. This crude man, his undiminished business success and his energy admired on all sides, humbles himself. In the end he permits his still youthful wife to deride him openly for his waning vitality. At home he submits to her unfailing and capricious reign of terror, which includes behaving whimsically and irrationally with the children and senselessly insulting his friends. In secret he tells his intimates that he believes his wife is ill. But he does not dare carry this insight to its conclusion.

The woman throws herself into local political activity. She makes speeches, is elected to the board of governors of a small association, travels about as a functionary, and gains some satisfaction in the exercise of political power in her small circle. Her husband supports her in her political ambitions and in the illusion that her influence is important. He permits her to travel about on business, neglect the house, do nothing about caring for the children, and escape almost entirely from his own influence. For a few years he tries behind her back to pick up the broken pieces, but he no longer allows things to come to open confrontation. Meanwhile, he loses by degrees what little was left of any perspective toward his wife's irrational development. He is simply unable to stand the tension of guarding himself even partially and covertly against her unrelenting demand for solidarity. His former halfhearted yes-saying has become automatic yes-thinking, and he is unable to recognize that in her hectic activity she is developing more and more pronounced signs of an illusionary querulousness. Her interests circle closer and closer around the supposed evil and inefficiency of other people, excluding everything except proofs of her own infallibility. Ever more frequently she provokes arguments with the authorities, acquaintances, and unsympathetic relatives. Through her paranoid, pretentious self-importance, she continually terrifies even her best-natured friends. The result is that she soon isolates herself even from her small circle of political influence.

As long as her husband, children, and servants obediently applaud her and, when called upon, fall into place in their mandatory roles as allies, the tensions within the family remain fairly well hidden. In this phase, the paranoid family configuration is practically complete: they sit together in a common fortress, sustained by the illusion of their own superiority, and make sallies against outsiders who are ostensible disturbers of the peace and their persecutors.

Two of the children begin to show resistance against the paranoid regime of their parents. At once their mother turns on them in a frenzy, as though she had run amok. It is unthinkable for her to release anyone from her narrow zone of influence. She must inflict prompt and vengeful punishment on those who disobey her. So she rages blindly against her two children. For years these two, despite their courageous opposition, are unable to escape from the magic circle of the querulous, hallucinatory system. At the same time, to their tremendous disillusionment, they are left in the lurch by their father, whose support they had secretly counted on. They are forced to recognize that in this hallucinatory atmosphere laden with aggression no discussion is possible—only a life-or-death battle or flight to an unattainable isolation.

In fact, later on, in the course of their education three of the children achieve at least partial freedom—constantly pursued, of course, by letters of reproach and advice from home. Despite the pressure to cooperate, this escape nevertheless produces a partial collapse of the paranoid system.

Within her reduced circle—her husband, two children, a distant relative full of compatible resentment, and a few dependent servants—almost all that remains to this aging woman as a unifying theme is the force of autosuggestion, the idea of her own splendor untainted by the slightest trace of self-critical doubt. There is further continuous denunciation of the enemy outside, for whom she invents all manner of spiteful punishments. Thus the remnant of the group solidifies in a "crazy" system of thought, induced by the mother's ideas of grandeur, illusions of persecution, and querulous hallucinations. It is the final phase in the paranoid process of self-destruction of a family that once seemed to be an ideal model of modern success.

The Sex Exterminator

The following case, too, involves the development of a neurosis in a modern couple. This time, however, it is not the woman who refashions reality in a paranoid manner. The man does so first, and the woman enters only secondarily into the neurotic ideology of her husband—until solidarity here, too, falls apart in the end.

A businessman lives in a state of extreme tension with his wife. The man, although only a little older than his wife, is verging on impotence, but he cannot accept it because his approach to life depends on not doubting his manhood and virility. He loves to have people fear him and submit to him. His young wife, too, at first fulfills this wish. She is awed by his imposing appearance and his energetic manner. Because of her sexual inexperience, she is initially unaware of his impotence. Her sexual deprivation becomes a problem only very gradually, and meanwhile the husband succeeds in warding off demands from his intellectually inferior partner by indoctrinating her with constantly larger doses of an ascetic ideology. At every opportunity he reviles the "destructive wave of sex" that is ushering in a cultural collapse. The absence of sexual principles among the young of today is the worst of all evils. His house, so he proclaims even on social occasions, will be kept pure and above reproach. His chronically unsatisfied wife, under the pressure of these threatening speeches, develops greater and greater feelings of guilt. After a few fruitless attempts at protest, she finally adopts for herself the anti-sexual ideology of her husband. In fact, she unconsciously develops a reaction formation, as a result of which she competes with her husband in reviling all exhibitions of sex in the mass media. After that, the marriage relationship becomes less tense. The pair join in a bellicose, anti-sexual ideology and find constant occasions to reassure each other of their solidarity by talking indignantly about "sexual filth." Through this identification with her husband's ideology, the woman escapes for the time being the danger of a catastrophic marriage battle. Moreover, the joint belligerent alliance ties up so much energy on both sides that neither of the two is aware of illness. The drying up of sexual intercourse is reinterpreted ideologically, although it is actually pathological. This reversal based on resentment characterizes in this instance the neurotic alteration of character in the married couple. Psychologically their paranoid falsification of reality can be understood as a generalized scapegoat strategy: they deny their own unsolved sexuality by projectively tracking it down and condemning it in the outer world.

As could be expected, their anti-sexual attitude influences the education of their only son. The boy turns out to be a well-behaved, quiet child especially concerned about cleanliness. But one day at the age of seven his parents find him in a small garden house engaged in examining the unclothed body of the five-year-old daughter of their neighbors. And he admits that he had urged this strip tease on the girl because he wanted to see her naked.

The parents take the incident as a catastrophe. The boy is spanked and immediately sentenced to several weeks' confinement in his room. His parents pay a visit of apology to their neighbors, parents of the girl. They treat their son's by no means uncommon investigation of female anatomy as a dreadful crime. But their expectation that the neighbors will share their moral indignation is sadly disappointed. The girl's parents react calmly and even try to soothe their horrified callers. The latter, however, will not allow themselves to be dissuaded from their sinister version of the incident; and in their eagerness to punish, they even go so far as to include their now morally suspect neighbors in their indignation. They feel themselves the heroes of a moral tragedy, innocent warriors for a pure world, persecuted by the devil and misunderstood into the bargain.

In the long run, however, their neurotic marriage arrangement loses its stability. At a carnival party the young wife succumbs to temptation with a young man and the affair develops into a lasting relationship between the two. The husband, who in the meantime has become much more dependent on the wife than his domineering manner would suggest, tolerates this extramarital relationship, though only with painfully suppressed bitterness. One day, however, he can bear it no longer and assails her with words and blows. The wife turns the tables on him and together with her friend accuses him of pandering, even reporting him to the police for this offense. She moves out of their home. The outcome is a prolonged, sensational divorce case.

Here, then, the common neurotic reaction formation has not served as a permanent foundation for the marriage character neurosis. The eruption of instinct on the part of the young wife destroys the solidarity of the defense system. The aggression, formerly controlled in a common ideological battle against the outside world, now breaks through right where it originally formed: in the conflict of the couple, who in their unreal anti-sex ideology had found only a deceptive refuge from their personal problems.

This example is instructive inasmuch as it clearly reveals the possible dynamic background of a family neurosis of the paranoid type. One can easily see how a marriage conflict, obviously hopeless from the start, can be covered over for a long time with the help of a common neurotic reaction formation and a jointly held process of idealization. As long as the "character change" prevails, there is an overly close agreement in the group—in contrast to the divisive processes typical of the symptom-neurotic family.

In many similar cases, moreover, a joint reaction formation proves strong enough to prevent the unmasking of the repressed marriage conflict. Then the paranoid family neurosis not only maintains its structure but sometimes even solidifies through continual elaboration of the joint defense system over the course of years or decades. If one wanted to be strict about it, one could reserve the description "paranoid family character-neurosis" simply for those cases in which the change in the family "group ego" has fixated itself in this manner. We believe, however, that one can go beyond this narrow definition and apply the description wherever a family endeavors to rid itself of a neurotic conflict, not through division into healthy and ill (symptom family), but the other way about: through closer unification by means of parallel reaction formations, projections, and idealization, no matter what degree of irreversibility the family character change may already have reached.

Dance Round the Ailing Angel

Another example of a paranoid family will serve to show that there is a variation of a comparatively harmless kind, harmless in that the prominent aggressive components of the cases mentioned before appear less clearly. In the following and similar instances, the family character change is in the direction of narcissistic isolation, a withdrawal into a private, illusory world of the family's own making. This limitation, however, does not give rise to continuous bellicose involvement with the surrounding world, as in the previous cases.

A revenue officer and his wife, a former saleswoman, have wanted a child for a long time. Finally a daughter, Marion, is born. It is a complicated birth. The umbilical cord becomes twisted around the infant's neck; breathing is slow in starting. After a few months, Marion suffers a series of convulsions, one after another. With medication, the attacks disappear. Marion is a delicate child, very timid and sensitive. She weeps easily, eats irregularly, and wakens easily at night. She is a trifle slow in learning to walk and speak. Her intelligence, insofar as it can be measured by tests, develops with some delay. But there are no further attacks of illness, and the doctors advise her parents to regard the child as healthy and to treat her as completely normal.

This advice is given because they have observed how Marion's parents behave toward her. Her father in particular is at pains to see that his daughter is watched over and cared for like a newly hatched chick. Returning from his office in the evening, he immediately examines her and inquires about the day's adventures. The minute she looks a trifle pale or does not eat properly, he suspects her mother of having done something wrong. On the other hand, he is filled with admiration and amazement at every new word the girl learns and at her first awkward scribblings with crayons. Her mother has to keep a daily record book; every discarded toy, every meaningless scrawl is carefully collected as though these were historical relics.

The mother suffers as Marion turns into a peevish and

defiant child. The little one is always able to get her way; again and again the mother, though annoyed, bows to her husband's educational principles. She is terribly afraid of being scolded by him, and in the course of time she becomes more and more doubtful about her critical feelings toward the child. And so by degrees she swings over completely to her husband's side. When he reproaches her for not having prevented Marion from falling on the sidewalk and bruising her leg, or being frightened by a dog so badly that in the evening she cannot go right to sleep, the mother swallows the reproaches without argument and condemns herself for her failure. Convinced that she must constantly do more for the child, she does not let Marion out of her sight for an instant or let her be tended by anyone else. She no longer visits and she receives in her home only such guests as will not disturb her constant, anxious, and submissive attachment to the child.

Her husband does everything possible to reinforce this attitude in his wife. He outdoes her in seeing that every desire of the child is fulfilled and he never finds fault with her highly irritating peculiarities. And so Marion likes to take refuge with her father; she complains if her mother ever refuses any wish or asks her for some kind of service. She can be sure that her father will rescue her satisfactorily.

The consequence of this steady admiration and pampering is that Marion gradually takes over control of the house. What she wants is done. Naturally, she does not want to go to kindergarten once she finds out that her wishes are not unquestionably followed by the other children, as they are at home. Her parents dare not take her to the dentist when she has tooth trouble; she has refused to go. Finally, she won't have any other children come to visit her, for she does not wish to concern herself with what interests them. Everything has to be arranged according to her will. She will play only with her parents' dog and with her toys. Her mother, too, must join in the game on demand; otherwise, Marion screams and goes on screaming until her mother relents. As might be expected, Marion eats only certain favorite foods. And she can be sure—with her father's support—that the menu conforms precisely to her wishes.

One may well ask how the parents can stand this painful submission to the little tyrant. This question stems from the supposition that the parents, like ordinary human beings, would refuse to allow their principal interests to be so cramped because of the selfishness of a child, but that supposition does not hold here. Her parents have completed a process of rearranging their ideas. To serve and to obey the delicate, susceptible child they have been given is their most consuming life interest. Nothing is so important to them as to gain approval in the eyes of their amazing darling. This leitmotiv, adhered to absolutely by the father but with still perceptible ambivalence by the mother, stands at the very top of the family hierarchy of values.

The deification of the child is rationalized in various ways, including of course her sickliness, as though she were one destined to die, one who for a brief period of life must be granted the greatest possible amount of happiness. Also, it is particularly the father's delusion that Marion is unique, a most extraordinary being of incredible preciousness. Thus ultimately it becomes a distinction to sacrifice one's own petty interests to the demands of this exceptional child. Of course, neither parent would think of using the word "sacrifice." In their eyes, especially in the father's, service to the child is so satisfying a task that every effort on her behalf is a matter of course.

Here the paranoid illness can be recognized. Certainly one is used to seeing the parents of an especially delicate or handicapped child overvaluing the child's virtues—a normal protective maneuver of the unconscious to maintain equilibrium. One persuades oneself that the sacrifices and efforts made for a difficult child of this sort are compensated for by the latent gifts that can be awakened in the child or, at the very least, the precious character traits that will be revealed in the future. These illusionary comforts sustain the parents and protect them from any inward protest or foreboding about the sickly child and, perhaps, from secretly wishing the child away. Conscience would forbid such ruthless thoughts. And so every occasion is used to create flattering illusions and to keep their concern for the child as unambivalent as possible.

In this case, however, the self-deception of the parents,

through the father's insistence, goes beyond the usual measure. The uncritical deification of the child to the point of complete self-surrender has taken on neurotic illusionary proportions. For the parents, the question is no longer: How can we help this ailing child to achieve a reasonably normal development? Instead, they ask: How can we inadequate parents in some measure fulfill the requirements of this marvelous angel? From here it is an easy step to protecting the girl from contact with her contemporaries. The parents do not want to be confronted with Marion's backwardness in development; they hold fast to the belief that the girl is far above her contemporaries in refinement, consciousness, and inner maturity. Compared to the others, she is not inferior but more splendid. Here they are quite simply constructing an illusion, a falsification of reality.

Typical, too, is the unalterability of their character-neurotic ideology. They have no trouble at all in disregarding the reasonable educational advice of doctors and of many relatives. If the child's doctor, for example, recommends that Marion be allowed to play freely with other children and that she should stop having only specially favored foods, the father summons up just enough self-control to meet with considerate silence what he considers abject ignorance. The mother, more impulsive, becomes involved in heated arguments with such advisers. She becomes agitated because she still has trouble maintaining the paranoid counterfeit reality. When her own unconscious doubts are stimulated from outside, she has to oppose them immediately and vigorously, out of fear that she might give in to these doubts and develop hostile feelings toward her daughter, thus losing the protective solidarity with her husband. And so this family preserves its "private world" against all outside criticism. And it is easy to see that this pampered, deified girl will have very slender chances of finding a place for herself in the world of true reality, which is so far removed from the pseudo-reality of her home.

How do such parents develop this massive, joint paranoid neurosis?

Certainly, general motives which could be described as common to the parents of all handicapped children play their part. In this case, however, quite special determinants are added.

The father is a physically weak but remarkably ambitious man who has had to suffer grievances repeatedly in the course of his life because of the rejection of his belligerent, expansive efforts. Even his mother disappointed him by being abrupt and harsh with him. In business he is constantly involved in disputes because of his arrogant behavior. Many reverses have deeply humiliated him, especially because of his need to dominate, but these have never altered his aggressive self-assertiveness. He married a much younger, childlike, less intelligent woman in the hope that her loving and submissive admiration would be his for as long as he lived. After a number of years of marriage, however, increasing tensions arose because of the young wife's strong resistance to his assuming absolute control.

The problems of the ailing child then provide the man with a chance to reestablish his position. He is aided in this by his wife's inclination to react to her daughter's illness with exaggerated feelings of guilt. As a child she once pushed her little sister off a wall, causing a concussion of the brain. Her stern parents had often reproached her with having almost killed her sister. Because of a strong feeling of envy for the sister, who was more favored than she, she felt unable to defend herself against these accusations. Finally she did actually hate her sister. Thus the reproaches she suffered from her parents were gradually transformed into chronic, gnawing self-reproach. To the present day, she had not freed herself from this unconscious self-hatred, and out of the unresolved conflict she now becomes the defenseless victim of her husband's accusations. She reacts as though the birth complications and the ensuing illness of her daughter were the consequences of her own shortcomings and she must make restitution for a disaster caused by her. And she must do this through the confessions of guilt and acts of expiation constantly demanded of her by her husband. Thus, through an unconscious repetition compulsion, she transfers in imagination her unresolved problem with her sister to her relations with her daughter.

Her husband, chief initiator of their joint submissive deification of the sick child, has in addition to reestablishing command over his wife another motive for the development of this abnormal ideology: he unconsciously identifies with the little girl. While his wife furnishes him with relief by assuming the role of scapegoat, he projects his "weak side" onto his daughter. Behind the façade of inexorably pugnacious man of power, he is meek and vulnerable, a wounded and mortified creature. This weak and defenseless side of him he now mirrors in his ailing daughter. In her he sees the duplicate of the thousand-times unjustly frustrated being that he secretly knows himself to be. But just as he violently overcompensates for his own weakness, so he must take care that this aspect of his daughter shall be repaired through effective defense mechanisms. This purpose is served first of all by reinterpreting her delicate health as something marvelous and admirable. And by compelling his wife as well as any guests in his house to pay homage to the dear little girl as though she were a higher being, he is also making restitution to himself for the many insults he has suffered. While he allows the spoiled little princess to lord it over everyone around, he enjoys—secretly identifying with her—the humiliation of the healthy and strong, at whose hands he has suffered so many defeats. On his mother, too, he takes belated, imaginary revenge. This is the additional meaning of his particular insistence that his wife subject herself to every wish of the child. His wife must expiate the wrongs he feels his mother did him.

These background motivations show that in the structure of this paranoid family neurosis aggressive components clearly play a part, although an outsider's first impression would be that the parents are especially loving, tender, and self-sacrificing. In actual fact, the idealized cult of the little angel rests on a typical case of resentment. Behind the unified reaction formation of the parents there lurks hatred from several sources: hatred of the mother toward her more favored little sister, hatred of the father toward his stern mother and all those who have tormented him in his business life—and lastly, of course, dissembled rage at the tyrannical little daughter herself, whom they adore as an angel in order not to have to hate her as an annoying little devil. Like the other paranoid families described, this one is able to protect the inner family realm from aggressive outbursts. The aggression is bound up in the distrustful encapsulating of the family against the surrounding world.

A paranoid family of this type usually withdraws into an illusionary, narcissistic, private world, but other paranoid families in which a bellicose, aggressive note is more strongly evident are often involved for decades in feuds and lawsuits with their neighbors. In times of strong political unrest, paranoid families easily commit themselves uncritically to one side or the other. Since their paranoid concept of life in any case inclines them to keep down their inner tensions by uniting against an outside enemy, times of political tension afford them the ideal opportunity to identify with an extreme political group, thus making use of the rivalry with an opposed political group to channel their own hostile impulses.

8

The Hysterical Family
CATCHWORD: THEATER

In some families, only one person develops symptoms of hysterical neurosis. In others, the whole family suffers something like a hysterical character change. A hysterical central figure organizes the family to meet his needs in such a manner that the others, who need not themselves be hysterically inclined, more or less participate in his hysterical arrangement. The central figure derives compensation thereby. And the rest of the family may feel no loss, although an outsider immediately notices that they are really denying their own personal identities, or failing to develop them, while they devote themselves more or less exclusively to the character parts assigned them by the hysterical stage manager. It can also happen that an individual rebels against the role intended for him, and in this conflict either falls ill with a neurosis or so frustrates his hysterical partner that the latter decompensates with accompanying symptoms. In that case, the hysterical "character-disturbed family" becomes a "symptom family." And there sometimes results a sequence of social symptom transferences such as has been described as characteristic of symptom families.

This type of family suffering from a hysterical character

alteration cannot be as succinctly described as can the character-neurotic or paranoid family. The forms of family hysteria are by comparison colorful and manifold. But one characteristic stands out in every case: the theatricality of family life. They all give performances for one another, or the whole family forms an ensemble and stages plays for the neighborhood. The important things are performance and effect.

The "artificiality" typical of the individual hysteric also characterizes the life of hysterical families. Anyone who simply wants to go his way in peace and live a realistic kind of life has a disturbing effect in a hysterical family. And so the other members and most of all the hysterical director attempt to irritate the "realist" until he joins the play, until he learns that he is not supposed to take himself and the others seriously and that they will not go on taking him seriously either. Something is said, something is done, some emotion is expressed—and it is by no means important whether one stands behind what one says, what one does or expresses. What is wanted is an immediate response that will serve as encouragement to go on playing. Anyone who attempted to reveal the illusionary, exaggerated, transient quality of this permanent theater would be branding himself as a spoilsport. And so the quiet, reserved members of a hysterical family often become involved at least to the extent of taking over the less important character parts in the family drama and also filling the role of stimulating, applauding onlookers—whereby they enter into the hysterical system anyway. In the great alternation between exhibitionism and voyeurism, the voyeuristic satisfactions are reserved principally for them.

You might say that the drama of the hysterical family is functioning at its best when the members reciprocally fascinate one another or are passively fascinated to such an extent that all of them experience adequate satisfaction in the process, and also if the family as a whole appears to the world outside as an attractive and successful ensemble.

In this way, then, a system of self-deception is pretty well completed, its purpose being to escape the manifold fears of isolation, weakness, and misery. Of course, any permanence of theatrical alienation from reality is continuously threatened with the intrusion of disillusionment. It is woeful indeed when one has to confront the chasm between the make-believe of the hysterical show world and genuine, "gray reality." The hysterical family constantly has to convince itself and its neighbors that its theater is the true world and that the world is only theater. If this faith collapses, nothing remains but depressive emptiness. In fact, the whole artificially constructed hysterical stage set is a nervously contrived defense system against the dangers of depression. And so again and again one sees depression break out in hysterical families when any sort of occurrence interrupts the illusionary play; for instance, the sudden death of the central figure on whose stage-managing ability the ensemble depended. Sometimes one sees a hysterical family that is still full of dramatic power and fascination suddenly collapse. This is often the first time friends on the outside realize how unreal and fragile was the base on which the family had staged its brilliant performances.

Splendor and Misery of a Show Ensemble

An expansive woman inclined to ostentation and exaggeration marries, after several unsuccessful affairs, a stately-looking man who is, however, psychically delicate and relatively frail. He is happy to allow himself to be managed by her in many ways. She sees to it that he dresses properly. Thanks to her many connections, she helps him advance in his career. But at the same time she requires for her peace of mind the assurance that he owes his success to her. She wants people to acknowledge and respect her husband. But these people must at the same time admire her for what she has made out of this man. And most important of all, her husband himself must take part in the game. He can assert himself only insofar as he acknowledges her rule. If he threatens the arrangement by exercising too much independence, the solicitous attitude of his hysterical wife turns suddenly to hatred. She is then quite capable of changing her protective attitude into sly intrigue against him: her husband must never forget that she alone has the power to build him up or tear him down. Only as the willing object of her stage management can he protect himself from the fear of worthlessness which she is able to keep alive in him by playing upon his profound self-doubt.

And so to this woman her husband represents principally a narcissistic complementary figure (chiefly, her "weak side"), but also to some extent a positive extension of herself because she hopes through him to assure herself of phallic virility, the absence of which she has never become reconciled to. This too is the reason that her marriage partner must permit her the illusion that it is really she who arouses, directs, and protects his masculinity.

Although to many observers the husband appears a wretched victim of the hysterical wife's tyranny, he is nevertheless completely responsible for his fate. He played his part in deciding on this hysterical marriage configuration. It is his decision not to try to overcome his self-doubts by means of his own strength or with the help of a psychotherapist but instead to rely upon a compensatory partner who can supply in abundance what he will not run the risk of developing. And so he delegates the role of his ideal (phallic-narcissistic) self—and thereby gives up asserting more strongly the corresponding desires in himself. As long as the man continues to live on good terms with his wife, he feels himself agreeably stimulated by her constantly entertaining, dramatic self-display and sheltered by her overindulgent protection. He can satisfy his secret vanity by participating in the admiration which she arouses on all sides. Finally, without any special exertion, he can regard himself as the envied victor in the contest with numerous suitors who, like him, are strongly attracted by this woman.

Of course this is only a pyrrhic victory. He knows better than anyone else that he is not the conqueror, not even the equal partner of his wife. If she sometimes allows him to give the appearance of a marvelous husband, this is only in order to lend luster to a prize possession. Systematically, she schools their three children for roles that will fit properly into her dramatic concept. The children, too, must be as striking as possible and effectively enlarge the family theatrical troupe. The children are rewarded for everything that impresses outsiders, that has an attractive effect—or that shocks, for that matter, or appears especially comic. The principal thing is that the children are not "boring" but rather that they are "interesting." They must be "sought after." Nothing annoys the mother more than the absence of an echo, than indifference on the part of the public; she is immediately assailed by fears of inferiority. For she is unable to derive confidence in her own worth from within herself but only from immediate response from without.

Her eldest son is a willing object of her managerial arts. She teaches him to comport himself as an attractive, charming boy, and she enjoys binding him to herself through her hysterical, seductive tactics, like a little gigolo. On the other hand, she inspires him with uncritical, grandiose fantasies. She promises that later on she will make him a great, powerful man, and this ambitious outlook soon plunges the boy into megalomaniac daydreams. Since, however, she carefully avoids encouraging his impulses toward autonomy, he remains relatively weak and dependent. It is completely safe for her to prophesy an impressive future for him, since she does not release him from his childhood bonds to her. On the contrary. The more Utopian and exaggerated the ideas of the future with which she bewilders his mind, the surer she can be of his servitude. For his genuine awareness of weakness must more and more convince him that only his mother can guarantee the realization of the dreams of greatness she has prophesied. Thus his role soon acquires characteristics similar to those of his father's.

The next oldest, a daughter, is a merry, unaffected child, quite guileless and frank. She becomes a problem to her mother because from the start she seems unsuited to understanding the concept of a hysterical role. She has a robust inner core. She says and does whatever occurs to her, bluntly and without calculating its practical effect. And so to fit her into the hysterical family ensemble without complications takes great effort on the part of the mother, who nevertheless finds a way: this daughter will be systematically exploited in the role of the "young innocent." The unspoiled directness of the child's expressions of feeling and opinion are greeted with much smiling applause. The little one becomes a kind of court jester, a clown figure. On social occasions she is encouraged to put on regular little performances, in which she is told to make the most of her comic gift for the entertainment of the guests. Naturally, this causes the girl to lose much of her naturalness and her innate self-confidence. She feels intuitively that they want to train her to act the role of herself, that nobody cares very much what she is, but only what effect she makes, indeed that no one really wants her to develop behind the mask of comedienne any sort of character that will have to be taken seriously. She is supposed to be and to remain simply the little "fool," naïve and a bit silly. As becomes painfully clear to her, there is nothing for her to do but immerse herself in this role and keep quiet about whatever else may be going on within her. This is the way they want her, no matter what, and this is the way she wins such friendly attention. Were she to attempt to break away—as would be essentially more appropriate to her completely unhysterical character—she would find herself in a state of helpless isolation that would be unendurable.

The younger daughter, at first, has an easier time of it. She is pretty as a picture, coquettish, and very much like her mother. This makes it easier for her mother to identify herself with the child. The mother encourages her to adopt all the techniques for seducing and fascinating people at which she herself is so thoroughly adept. The sight of the little girl enchants everyone, and the mother enjoys this—naturally, she considers the success of her "duplicate" her own success. In any case, this daughter soon takes her place on the family stage in a supporting role, which, to be sure, serves to make the mother seem even more brilliant in her leading part. The daughter is made ready for a splendid marriage. And in fact she does marry, very young, an entrepreneur of noble birth who—need it be said?—simultaneously pays the mother all the expected homage. The son-in-law soon goes bankrupt. His young wife, dependent on public success, leaves him. Many initially promising friendships come to nothing and in the end she falls victim to alcohol.

Before this, however, her mother has met with a fatal accident—with catastrophic after-effects, especially for the husband.

Many expected that this man, who had dangled like a marionette from his wife's fingers and suffered a thousand humiliations, would after the first sorrow at his loss be able to demonstrate his abilities more freely than before. Every superficial observer had had the impression that only the presence of the domineering wife kept the husband from acting more self-confidently and ambitiously. Instead of this, the man collapses completely and never recovers from the blow. Stripped of initiative, he simply vegetates, and only the intense supportive concern of his older children and several other relatives keeps him from losing his hold completely. Finally he is put in a Swiss sanitarium, where in his depressed helplessness he cannot get along without constant nursing care.

In retrospect, his fate illustrates clearly the compensatory function which the hysterical family configuration fulfilled. As long as the hysterical ensemble was intact, its members supported one another reciprocally: the husband as a safe playmate, a decorative prince consort, and obedient devotee of his wife had helped to keep her stable. She in turn had given him support, direct protection, and stimulation, and at the same time the opportunity—as substitute for his phallic narcissistic ego-ideal—to share as a kind of silent partner in the enjoyment of her successes. Now he is left behind as a helpless and depressed, truncated creature. He might truthfully say of himself that he has lost "his better half." For this was exactly what his wife was to him, and now at his age he no longer has the resiliency to make up for the amputation he has suffered.

Here in a most general way we have one of the chief problems of the hysterical family configuration. The system of roles is designed according to the needs of the dominating central figure. The roles of the other members of the family derive their meaning from their relation to the role of the principal actor, who at the same time coordinates the collective by his direction. For him, and according to his conception, each of the others plays his part, at times in a successfully "concerted" harmony. If this central figure drops out, however, a catastrophe is usually inevitable. The toll is now exacted for the fact that the hysterical family game prevented the individual participants from sustaining their own personal identities or, for that matter, developing identities of their own at all. They are like actors who no longer know how to realize any part of their own being outside the limits of a memorized role. After the bond of their hysterical play-acting has been broken, the various individuals suddenly feel like functionless fragments. It is only after an almost intolerable isolation that the truncated quality of their former existence and the absence of a personal identity become terrifyingly clear. The fear of nothingness, of emptiness, drives them to despair.

As a rule, those who played marginal parts in the family theater—the younger daughter, for instance—have the easiest time in coming to terms with the new situation. The smaller roles, after all, allow some freedom for a degree of self-realization, whereas the persons closest to the central figure must now pay dearly for having been drawn into the intimate circle. Earlier, they had the feeling of being enriched by his special attention—now they see that they had simply been emptied to an extraordinary degree, or that they had emptied themselves.

This example indicates, moreover, that a hysterical character-neurotic family can transform itself into a symptom-neurotic family if the solidarity formed by the hysterical system falls apart. The theatrical ensemble breaks up into a loose assembly of individuals, one or more of whom decompensate with neurotic symptoms. Conspicuously manifest are depressive characteristics which formerly were—quite literally—kept out of sight by the temporarily functioning collective hysteria.

It is not only the absence of the managerial person that can seriously threaten the balance of a hysterical family ensemble; the loss of other members can have a similar effect. Even the rather passive, reserved members sometimes have an important stabilizing function in the family, which may be fully recognized only if one of them suddenly breaks away from the company.

You Can't See in the Dark

A couple with one small daughter are entirely dominated by the highly active, hysterical wife. She is famous citywide because of her enormous social acquaintanceship and her sparkling personality. At all celebrations and other public occasions she is numbered among the prominent persons present. At her house, one party follows another. In the course of time she assembles an impressive following of people whom she is able to entertain and fascinate with constantly new inspirations. Her pretty little daughter, who quickly acquires the affected airs of a child star, increases the distinction of the house. The husband gives rather the impression of a handsome supernumerary who is important only to complete the décor for the appearance of the prima donna. Unprotesting, he tolerates his wife's many temporary as well as the more prolonged flirtations with the most varied admirers. On occasion, she practically has to force him to come out of himself a bit at parties, to call attention to himself. After all, he must not give the impression of being a completely boring halfwit. Nevertheless, most friends of the family consider the husband a negligible quantity, a simple appendage to his magnificent wife.

A day comes when the family has to move, for professional reasons. And before they are settled in the new city, the husband has to go to a sanitarium for a year because of lung trouble. Thereupon the wife, apparently still bursting with health and vitality, suddenly collapses. She weeps for hours at a time, can no longer sleep, and rushes about in a kind of panic. Her daughter can do nothing to please her. She reduces the servants to complete confusion by constant petty criticism. She would like to take flight back to her former city and there seek refuge with one of her old friends. Suddenly she feels that she can no longer go on living. One physical symptom after another appears: abdominal pains, gall-bladder pains, shooting pains in the breast, to which are added a particularly hectic nervousness and regular anxiety states. Her condition is what is known as a nervous breakdown. After consultation with three doctors, she finds refuge in a nursing home and there, after several months, she gradually recovers.

In her conversation with the doctor, it becomes clear how greatly all observers underestimated the importance of the quiet husband for the wife's equilibrium. He had been quite wrongly regarded as a completely dispensable or exchangeable appendage. This had always been his role in public, but privately his wife was deeply in need of his support. Only under the magic protection of his patient and completely dependable reassurance can the little girl, who in reality she has always remained inwardly, sustain her imposing stellar role. Not one of her many admirers knows that every evening she has to hear several times from his lips that she has played her part well. And like a poor little child, she has to allow herself to be warmed and pampered by him in order to summon up strength for her next performance. If she dominates all conversation with the greatest self-confidence and expresses eccentric opinions while her husband barely opens his mouth, once they are alone together she listens with childish submissiveness to his opinions. Thus it comes to a simple exchange of roles in private. There he is suddenly for a while the powerful wise father and she the uncertain weak child who must gain strength from him in order next day to play the great role of herself. Hence her helplessness and brainlessness once her husband is sent to a sanitarium.

The principal in a hysterical family neurosis, if he loses his partner, generally has better compensatory opportunities than, in the reverse case, the other members have when the central person drops out. In addition to husband or wife, the central person usually has other supporters in reserve. His ability to adapt to substitute partners is often quite remarkable. The hysteric, for example, does not cling nearly as close to a specific person as does someone of a depressive structure. In the foregoing example, the change of residence certainly plays a part as an increased difficulty for the hysterical wife. After all, she had had no time to provide herself in her new home with reserve partners.

This last case demonstrates that the hysterical family configuration not only can be easily shaken out of its pattern from within—through the loss of a member—but is threatened from outside as well, especially where supporting outside relationships disappear through a change of residence or other circumstances. The hysterical family immediately feels seriously insecure when it no longer has around it "an audience interested in drama." It has vital need of the atmosphere of a theatrical world. In fact, one of the principal distinguishing marks of the hysterical family character is that it is to a high degree dependent on outside encouragement. In the long run, it cannot continue to produce from within itself the impulses and stimuli that are necessary to keep the hysterical drama going. Only a sympathetic audience can assure the permanent and necessary theater atmosphere.

For this reason, one hysterical family can be seen happily joining forces with another. They alternatingly provide satisfaction for each other. Each family in turn plays for or applauds the other. They lend themselves to the usual small hysterical sensations. They find each other "mad," "devastating," "fantastic." Occasionally, "impossible" as well. But since they need each other, they always get together again. Finally, the small brawls and scandals between hysterical families are largely stage thunder and far from unpleasant as a titillation of the nerves. In any case, hysterical families strive endlessly to preserve for each other the illusion that their exalted artificial life style is the greatest. And together they deprecate the unhysterical world as lacking in comprehension, as philistine, dull, witless. They have need of this resentment-reaction formation because of the chronic fear, already described, that they might be wrong in their belief in the validity of their hysterical as-if world. This inclination of hysterical groups to perform together smooths the way for the emergence of hysterical subcultures, such as one sees, for example, widespread in relatively pure form among many movie, TV, and radio people.

A true paradise of the hysterical life style has been offered recently by fashionable resorts skillfully designed to meet the needs of an exclusively hysterical clientele. Here all is play, exhibition, and voyeuristic applause. Mountains and lakes become simply stage sets for big and little mimes playing the roles of themselves and living on the significance they impute to and derive from their factitious theater world. A pure culture of hysterical illusionism—intoxicating for the hysterics collectively; for the nonhysteric, comic, uncanny, irritating—impressions that can be found strikingly reflected in some of Tati's films.

Admittedly, hysteria is not simple make-believe, false tinsel, overcompensation for emptiness and depression or other psychopathological states. Certainly, in some extreme social situations, it appears simply silly—or deplorable. And in a clinical case, it unquestionably needs the care of a doctor as a condition requiring therapy.

But, naturally enough, hysteria has a completely different side, which in this clinical-psychopathological discussion can be mentioned only incidentally. Aspects of hysteria show themselves in various social fields—an interesting area of study for sociologists preschooled in psychoanalysis—as entirely productive, creative forces. In proper combination with other elements, "hysterical traits" can prove highly creative. Here one is likely to think only of the artistic fields. In any area where life is trying to take on new forms, it can make use of some of the fantasy peculiar to hysterics and of their continuous impulse to rethink the commonplace in original ways and to restage it freshly and creatively. Naturally, just as the anxiety neurotic's fear of taking risks and exaggerated emphasis on safety can easily result in arid rigidity, so hysteria, with its tendency to lose itself in fantasy, threatens the preservation of peaceful and realistic continuity. Nevertheless, without its compensatory characteristics, we would live in a duller, less colorful world.

9

Family Therapy and Family Counseling
EVOLUTION, USES, PROCEDURES

Like every other branch of medicine, psychotherapy for a long time concerned itself only with individuals. If several members of a family were involved in a psychic problem, the family—either alone or with the help of a doctor—tried to determine who was the *real patient* and should receive treatment. If several family members involved in the conflict needed therapy, then as a rule each had his or her own therapist. All branches of traditional medicine have clung tenaciously to the model of an exclusively bipolar doctor-patient relationship. Once a person became a patient, the rest of the family automatically fell into the category of relatives.

In the traditional medical scheme, relatives have an entirely different relationship to the doctor from that of the patient. They are supposed to help the doctor diagnose the patient's illness and aid in its successful treatment. In some cases, they are asked about the early stages of the illness and the doctor advises them about appropriate nursing care for the sick person. The relatives then, in respect to the doctor, are not recipients of help but co-workers. They are expected to serve the welfare of the patient without reference to any needs of their own and to follow the doctor's directions systematically and intelligently. These directions are generally of a pragmatic kind. And so the relatives are reduced more or less to being an ill-informed attendant. Under the professional seal of secrecy, the doctor reveals only a minimal part of his knowledge about the patient.

This triangle of roles, patient-doctor-relative, as institutionalized in our culture is based on an assumption that is usually valid in organic illness but much less so in psychic disturbances. The assumption is that the relative himself is healthy and has nothing to do with the illness of the patient. But the foregoing chapters have demonstrated in detail that this assumption is not tenable in psychological medicine. In many cases, the relatives of a psychogenically disturbed individual are not psychically healthy themselves. And their own psychic difficulties can be causally intertwined with the problem of the person who presents himself as the patient.

In such cases, forcible interference is required to set up the triangle of roles. If the relatives are themselves neurotic and their neuroses support, at least unconsciously, that of the patient, then even in the face of moral reproach they will not willingly lend themselves to the role of therapeutic helpers. Instead, out of unconscious compulsion, they will tend to support the treatment only partially; that is, insofar as their own neurotic needs are not frustrated by it.

The dilemma of psychotherapists who are intent on pursuing only the bipolar method of treatment is so obvious that one wonders how in the world psychological therapy could have been inflexibly modeled on organic medicine for so long. Countless times, psychotherapy has come to grief because the patient's family were secretly and successfully allied not with the therapist against the neurosis but with the neurosis of the relative against the therapist. One can hardly guess at the number of mothers who have sent their children to child psychotherapists and have so prejudiced the children against the doctor's advice that no form of psychotherapy could make headway against them.

Why, then, was the two-person arrangement retained so long and so rigidly as a matter of principle?

One reason was mentioned in the third chapter. Psychoanalysis, despite the Oedipus-complex theory, was originally a psychology of the individual exclusively; hence its application for so long a time entirely to the inner conflicts of individuals. A number of other considerations on the part of both patient and therapist also enter in. The principal wish of a neurotic patient in many cases is to have the therapist all to himself. He wants to escape, at least in psychotherapy, the envy and jealousy conflicts from which he suffers at home or in his business life. He believes that he can accept unambivalently only a therapist for whose favor he does not have to compete. The psychotherapists, for their part, know that the treatment of a single individual is generally less irksome than working with the compounded problems of a whole family group. It is easier to gain an overall view of a single person's difficulties than of the interacting conflicts of a number of individuals in a family. Also, it is easier to withstand the emotional transference of a single patient and work through it than to deal with the complex undergrowth of emotions of an entire group disturbed by neurotic tensions. In individual therapy there is no danger of being involved in a tug-of-war between opposed family members or even being exposed to the united defense of an entire family. It is perfectly true that in individual therapy one comes to feel the reactions of the rest of the family.* And as a result of these reactions, the therapy may in certain circumstances end in failure. But at least the relatives, who are often regarded as a nuisance, are not present in the consulting room. And one can even invoke ethical principles, especially professional discretion, for keeping them away.

In any case, there is no lack of reasons, though they may be only partially justifiable, to explain the prolonged continuance of the exclusively two-person system of treatment. Some thirty-five or forty years ago there was briefly a stronger interest, in psychological medicine, in broadening the sociopsychological basis of psychoanalytical treatment. At that time, various analysts felt it was inadequate to deal exclusively with the inner problems of the individual.

---

* Freud considered it natural and unavoidable that at some point the relatives of a patient would develop opposition to the psychoanalysis of one of the family.[28]

Burlingham[13] and Bornstein[9] were among the first to concern themselves with the unconscious influences of mothers on their children, and as early as 1932 Burlingham recommended, as a result of her observations, that mothers should be included in child analyses. She described the difficulties and also the fundamental advantages of combined treatment. Oberndorf[65, 66] and later Mittelmann[64] were pioneers in the field of research and treatment of neurotic marriage problems. Oberndorf apparently was the first to treat married couples systematically and psychoanalytically, and he reported on this in 1933 and more extensively in 1938. The psychoanalytical congress in Nyon in 1936 had as one of its principal topics family neuroses and neurotic families. Laforgue, Leuba, and Aichhorn mainly discussed pathogenic relationships between married couples and between parents and children.

It is hard to explain why it was another twenty years before direct research and therapy of disturbed group processes in the family were more vigorously pursued. Today we see that those pioneers opened the way to one of the most important fields for the broadened application of psychoanalysis. In the last few years alone, the literature on family dynamics and family therapy has grown so rapidly that it is difficult to keep up with it. In the psychopathology of children and young people, family therapy is now essential. In particular, the treatment of families with young schizophrenics has made astonishing advances and proved of far-reaching significance, thanks to the trail-blazing labors of the disciples of Lidz and Fleck,[60, 62, 63] Boszormenyi-Nagy,[10] Jackson,[52, 53] Wynne,[86, 95] and others. In addition to therapy for parent-child problems, interesting modern procedures for the treatment of marriage difficulties have been developed. Here, following Oberndorf and Mittelmann, principally Dicks,[19, 20] Ackerman,[1, 2] Greene,[43] Brody,[12] Watson,[92] and Rodgers[80] opened up new paths. In this one field alone, the literature has proliferated in recent times. A survey made by Sager[82] mentions no less than seven different forms of analytically oriented marriage therapy which were being practiced at the time. To be sure, it is not yet known which of the new methods will retain their value and which may turn out to be simply preliminary experiments.

That marriage therapy is mentioned in the same breath as family therapy of young schizophrenics indicates what a heterogeneous area is covered by the concept of family therapy. It embraces clearly distinguishable constellations that can be treated: married couples, parents with one child, parents with several children, families including grandparents. Married couples are treated singly and also in groups of three to five couples.[44, 69, 70] The therapy of parental groups—carried on concurrently with separate treatment for the children—serves simultaneously to clarify difficulties in marriage and in schooling. There is family treatment with one, two, or three therapists. Finally, the various members of a family can be treated in a collective session (conjoint therapy), in separate sessions but with the same therapists (concurrent therapy), or with different therapists who collaborate with one another (collaborative therapy). Experiments are also being made in alternating separate sessions with different therapists and collective sessions of members of a family with their own therapists. Recently, in a number of places, entire families have been admitted at once into psychiatric clinics and treated while living there.[55] Because of the great variety in the composition of the groups treated, the difficulty of the technical arrangements, and the experimental character of many of the evolving methods, it is not simple to formulate enlightening generalities about family therapy.*

It is clear, however, that the phrase "family therapy" does not mean a single, definite, therapeutic-technical arrangement, but rather a number of relatively different methods. All these methods have the same subject matter and goal. Their object in every case is a family conflict instead of solely an individual inner conflict. And the goal is the working out of this conflict as thoroughly as possible; in any case, its partial solution. In this sense, Haley and Hoffmann[46] say: "Because of the variety of ways families are treated, one cannot call family therapy simply a new method of treatment; it is a new way of conceptualizing the cause and cure of psychiatric problems."

* Good summaries of several concepts and methods of treatment are to be found in Boszormenyi-Nagy and Framo: *Intensive Family Therapy*,[10] and Haley and Hoffmann: *Techniques of Family Therapy*.[46]

We are not quibbling here about definitions but pointing out an important difference between family and individual therapy, which even practicing family therapists and counselors often find it hard to appreciate. In fact, this difference implies a *radical* rethinking on the part of the therapist, and not merely a change in his formal relations with the patient, for instead of individual patients he is treating the other members of the family simultaneously or collectively. The decisive step in reorientation consists in this: that one recognizes and deals with an anxiety, a depressed mood, or some other symptom not as the attribute of an individual but as the characteristic of a family group. For what purpose does the family use this ailment? What was the initial cause of the problem, and how is the family dealing with it now? Is the family trying to rid itself of the conflict by means of an inner division? Is it trying to suppress it through united denial and by projecting it outward? Is it taking any steps to cure itself? Is it restructuring itself in such a way that a symptom bearer will be eliminated? Is the family arranging for aid from the outside because of its feeling of helplessness? Does the family expect from the therapist finally chosen that he will impose order like a father, belatedly fulfill disappointed, passive desires like a mother, or that he will fail as arbiter and be quickly cast out as the scapegoat? What other expectation does the family have of the therapist?

The family therapist must try to clarify all this to determine how best to connect into the disturbed inner communication of the family group, and above all to provide help so that it will not turn out to be one-sided but will benefit the whole family. This kind of sociopsychological appraisal of the diagnosis, the pathogenesis, the probable prognosis, and also of one's own therapeutic function is the criterion for deciding whether to propose family therapy or not. Out of all this there emerges secondarily the question of what technical arrangement is to be adopted in each case. The arrangement to be sought is the one that seems best suited to the particular family problem. Ackerman, one of the most important American pioneers in the field of family therapy, gives this rule: "Treatment must be problem-oriented, not technique-oriented."

Flexible, workable arrangements serve to make true family-therapy work possible. They are not synonymous with the work. No one can say that he is a family therapist simply because, for example, he treats married couples together, or groups of married couples, or parents and children. What he must establish is that he is able to see and treat as a whole a particular marriage problem or a parent-child problem. This does not follow automatically from the fact that he collects several members of a family on chairs in front of him. Actually, a sociopsychological experiment can easily miscarry. And with an inexperienced or inexpert therapist, the family group may suddenly break up into competing individual patients or—in the language of the older tradition—into a division of "patients" and "relatives." Naturally, at the beginning, problems of transference occur. But they must be attended to immediately, so that divisions of this kind are not inadvertently stimulated and fixated. Otherwise, behind the façade of a family-therapy arrangement, nothing but the old individual treatment takes shape. Resistance by the family or incapacity on the part of the therapist has kept the family problem from being analyzed in all its parts, and so makes adequate treatment impossible.

In properly conducted family therapy, the family itself is the patient. The ailment of a single individual cannot be the only object of therapy any more than a local symptom of the analysand in an individual psychoanalysis can be the only object. The ailment of the family has in a sense its pathophysiological substratum in the disturbed communication, the disturbed dialogue, of the group. The dialogue has been disrupted or fragmented through intrafamily division (in a symptom family); or instead of becoming distorted, it has become thematically narrowed, illusionarily "mad," or hysterically empty (in a character-neurotic family). It is on this failure in communication that family therapy must focus.

A psychoanalytical examination of a family can show that one of its members is in a psychological sense already living apart from the rest of the family. (This will be seen, for instance, in the case history in chapter 13.) But it is characteristic of this sort of family neurosis that the fact that one member has moved all his personal attachments outside the family has not been realized. In such a situation this "marginal figure" may not be persuaded to take an active part in family therapy, so only the other people in the group can be treated. For other, objective reasons as well, the members of a family may not all offer to take part in therapy; perhaps only two or three who have a problem in common may do so. It may be a fairly limited marriage problem of the parents in which the children are involved only peripherally through sympathy. Treating the married couple alone without the children may then be sufficient. Under the circumstances, one hopes that the children will recover automatically as soon as their parents have learned to handle their marital conflict more successfully.

Frequently, too, one sees a somewhat limited mother-child conflict that can be handled without extensive involvement by the father. This is the case if the father does not influence the mother-child neurosis to any appreciable extent by his behavior. To be sure, one must always take full account, in diagnostic considerations and therapeutic planning, of the children in a parent neurosis, of the father in a mother-child neurosis, and of the mother in a father-child neurosis. And as a rule, it is useful to have a conversation at least once with such less-involved family members and at the end to leave them with some advice. But they cannot share or may not need to share in the intensive treatment. It may turn out in the course of a close appraisal that the seemingly marginal character of a family member is the result of reversible expulsion tactics being practiced by part of the family. It would perhaps be more sensible, then, to include this already half-severed part of the family in the direct therapy. Otherwise, one might in certain circumstances be unwittingly cooperating with the family in its maneuvers to eject this person, thereby causing harm.

Naturally, there are often outside reasons—business obligations, household duties that cannot be postponed, and many other possible obstacles—which prevent now this member, now that one, from participating in the family therapy. Again and again, one may have to do without a participant in the therapeutic arrangement.

In each case, however, it remains to be seen whether the overt reason for the absence is not in reality inwardly motivated. One is often astounded by the ingenuity and zeal by which a person makes sure he takes part in therapy, if his motivation is strong enough. The therapist, therefore, should not be too quick to accept excuses if he feels that a particular family member must be drawn into the therapy. Often, after a number of meetings, an arrangement can be reached after all, if an appropriate relationship of confidence is established.

Specialists are not agreed on how many persons need be involved in a treatment for it to qualify as family therapy. Some feel that work with just one member of the family may be called family therapy if the core of the treatment is the problem of the whole family; whereas Sager calls it family therapy only when three or more persons are involved. Most specialists concur that work with childless couples should be considered family therapy. All group-oriented treatment, after all, is closely related, whether two, three, or more persons in the family are involved. And however varied the forms of treatment may be, they have in common their difference from classical individual therapy, and this is the criterion.

Yet problems of definition crop up that a psychoanalyst may not expect. Is family therapy, for example, applicable only to families in the legal sense? What about the family of an unmarried couple? A therapist encounters people who constitute a family but who live without any communication, as though a world apart, and would never cooperate with each other in family therapy. On the other hand, he sees individuals who legally are not considered of a family but who are in fact a tightly knit family and in the event of a conflict can be cured together as a family. For the therapist, the decisive criterion is the diagnostic and therapeutic applicability of the family-therapy model. In other words, he judges principally by the psychosocial structure of the group, not its legal status. The family-therapy research group established by Sager in New York puts it this way: "Our definition of family includes a 'couple (married, separated, living in common-law marriage, living together, or planning to live together) with or without

. children, or any group of close relatives comprising at least three persons capable of participating verbally in a family session . . .' These persons need not live under one roof. Emotional involvement with one another is the primary criterion." This pragmatic orientation has in general held good. After all, family therapy does not mean treatment of the family as an institution but treatment of a group of individuals who share a common problem.

It is true that family therapy is often in conflict with relevant legal formalities. Frequently, there is a close connection between complications based on family legal rights and conflicting psychosocial realities. One encounters this in extramarital pregnancies, adultery, divorce proceedings, child care after divorces, etc. Symptoms resulting from psychic processes may bring about judgments on the legal level that are of such importance for the course of family-therapy treatment that the therapist must keep the legal aspect constantly and seriously in mind. To keep in mind, however, does not mean to be dependent on it. An analytic family therapist is not a guardian of institutions, or an agent of legal or moral standards. For this reason, he applies with relative looseness the just discussed, broadly based concept of the family, consciously subordinating the legal factors to the psychological ones.

One last problem of definition: family counseling—how is this distinguished from family therapy?

A recent conference of specialists was unable to give a clear-cut answer to this question. The concept of therapy in the sense of curative treatment has a specific legal position in Germany. Therapy can be practiced only by doctors, doctors' aides, or medical assistants. And so, to begin with, this much is clear. According to law, educational advisers, marriage counselors, social workers, psychologists can act only as advisers to families, not as therapists.

But the facts are more complicated than legal regulations might lead one to believe. Since for a long time medicine devoted itself almost exclusively to organic illnesses and neglected emotional disturbances, other professions—fortunately—filled the gap. Thus the number of psychologists who after psychoanalytical training are functioning expressly as psychotherapists is increasing—and much good has come of it. Particularly in family work, one finds educational counselors, social workers, and psychologists who, as a result of good practical training, conscientious study of the literature, and special aptitudes, provide a form of family care that, measured by its thoroughness and effectiveness, can certainly be called "therapy." Much more so, in fact, than the purely pragmatic practice of many doctors in family situations, totally lacking as it is in conceptual foundations. Yet a doctor is entitled to describe as "family therapy" a dilettantish "good talking to" which fulfills none of the criteria of scientific treatment. On the other hand, a social worker thoroughly schooled in case work would be legally guilty if he were to describe as therapy a months-long labor with a problem family carried out conscientiously from a psychological point of view.

Here, once more, legal classification proves an unreliable guide to reality. And it is an equally unreliable signpost to the future. One trend can be clearly seen today. Family therapy, unquestionably on the verge of significant development, will take only a small number of its recruits from the professional group that supposedly has a monopoly on therapy; that is, the medical profession. Greater consideration, a better education, and broader legalization are owed to everyone engaged in clinical-sociopsychological projects and to gifted psychologists and social workers. A reform movement is called for. But the psychoanalyst, in particular, does not underestimate the barriers—particularly in set attitudes—that such a reform movement will have to overcome to succeed.

Society will make up its mind to provide adequate assistance in the struggle against psychic damage only when it discards its misconception that psychic injuries are faults rather than illnesses. The gradual conquering of this prejudice will also make it possible for people to call qualified psychological or sociopsychological therapeutic procedures by their right name and to recompense them accordingly.

In anticipation of this change, "family therapy" will be used here to cover all activities related to systematic family dynamics and aimed at curing family disturbances. Many of those who today can only consider themselves counselors may in fact follow this book on family therapy more easily than the majority of legitimate doctors trained for therapy just in the natural sciences.

From a practical point of view, in any case, the distinction between counseling and therapy is vague, since thorough psychological family counseling does not differ essentially from "brief therapy." Better than any attempt at a formal definition, the case history in chapter 15 should show how closely related therapy and counseling are; even the freer, less systematic, and often more rapidly completed work of counseling involves the same subtle and precise understanding of family conflict as the procedure which we are accustomed to call therapy in the stricter sense.

10

Which Families Can Be Helped by Family Psychotherapy?

One has to agree with Mittelmann,[64] who stated in 1941: "Neurotic circular interpersonal reactions are never absent in any well established neurosis." It is fascinating to study psychosocial disturbances in the light of our new knowledge of family dynamics. One is easily tempted to make family diagnoses everywhere and to experiment with family therapy. In fact, the pioneers in this field found that the concept of family therapy gave access to many and varied psychic ills. "In principle," as Ackerman,[2] one of the most experienced American family therapists, summed it up, "family therapy has a wide range of applicability to all classifications of psychiatric disorder, to all degrees of mildness or severity of such disorder, but it must be flexibly modified to accommodate to different conditions." And further: "It can be helpful in psychiatric disorders in which the interpersonal and social determinants loom large, in such conditions as acting out types of disturbance, sociopathic behavior, neurosis, psychosomatic crisis, and functional psychosis. In marital disorders and in disturbances of parent-child relationships, it is especially effective." Along with Ackerman, most family therapists emphasize the variety of application rather than the limits of the new method. Here, undoubtedly, some element of "discoverer's enthusiasm" is at play. With so new a method, it is understandable that there should be a lack of scientific criteria for accurately estimating its prospects as compared to other methods of treatment. Still, it is gratifying, precisely on scientific grounds, that, at the present time, experiments in family therapy are being conducted over a wide field to determine, through coordinated comparative testing, where this type of treatment accomplishes more and where it accomplishes less. Various study groups are systematically testing the effectiveness of family therapy, taking into diagnostic account differences in age, sex, race, economic status, and the expectations of the patients.

In the last ten to fifteen years, certain conclusions have been reached about the particular potentialities of family therapy as compared to other psychotherapeutic treatment.

1. It is a positive indication in family therapy that the various persons who take part have a common problem that makes it reasonable for them to work together, though only, perhaps, after a preparatory phase. The common element can, of course, consist in everybody's helping one member of the family free himself gradually from the rest of the group and become self-sufficient. Accordingly, Wynne[95] names as the first field of activity for a common family therapy, as practiced at the National Institutes of Health in Bethesda, the separation problems of the young. The other members of the family often suffer as much as or more than the young person himself in the crisis of parting. Wynne's experience has been that it can be very useful to consider these problems with the entire family, though, of course, effective individual therapy can also be carried on with the adolescents.

A couple quarreling and on the verge of divorce may still benefit from a family therapist. Their common problem can in fact be that, though both see the futility of continuing the marriage, they are so closely knit as a result of their neuroses that they dare not try a separation. The sick portion of the ego in each person is so entangled in a sort of paradoxical symbiosis with the other that, without help, both of them would rather wear each other down completely than let go. Marriage therapy may help both decide to risk the long-overdue separation and go through with it without attacks of anxiety.

2. An individual is involved in such deep, specific dependency on one or more members of the family that he is not able in analysis to shoulder his difficulties alone. In individual therapy he would not be able to stand the tension of the therapeutic transference relationship without symbiotically clinging with intenser regression to the person in the family with whom he is most deeply involved. He would not have the strength to confront his inner conflicts without a refuge of that sort. This holds true for a great many children and also for not a few adults with specific dependency problems. In such cases, the more involved the other family member is in the dependency relationship, the more family therapy is needed.

The next question, of course, is whether the stronger member of the family is willing to cooperate in joint therapy. Often, this willingness does not come spontaneously. If an individual is compensating for the pressure of an inner conflict by staging and maintaining a particular form of family neurosis, then he certainly will not give it up without something in return. A mother suffering from anxiety neurosis, for example, who has learned to lessen her latent fears through an overprotective clinging to her child, will not give the child more freedom unless one can show her a better way to free herself from her fears. And a sociopathic father who is able to protect himself from his subterranean self-hatred by means of scapegoat tactics will not easily consent to set free the family members trained for scapegoat roles through skillfully inspired feelings of guilt. That is, unless one puts him in a position to relieve in some other way his constantly threatened inner equilibrium.

It is by no means impossible to provide the individual who manages the family neurosis with a way to free himself and stop misusing dependent family members. First of all, the suspicion must be dispelled that, as principal culprit in the family neurosis, the person concerned will be viewed without sympathy and denounced. His fears, to be sure, would not be unfounded. He secretly knows that, as a result of his psychosocial behavior, he has on his conscience the neurotic dependency of one or more of the persons in his family. It might well be the psychotherapist's intention to deprive him of his victim, or at least to build resistance against him, thus isolating him. Perhaps, too, more than once, doctors have labeled this person an "undesirable relative" and with a dependent family member as patient have taken sides against him.

A family member who is used to ridding himself of inner tension by exploiting a partner requires at first an entirely different therapeutic approach from a dependent person who from the beginning presents himself in the role of a weak patient in need of help. The domineering person comes to the therapist with the "patient," if he appears at all of his own accord, in the role of normal companion. Whether the dependent patient is a child, an adolescent, or a marriage partner, the domineering family member usually presents himself immediately as an unquestionably superior person. He generally makes it clear that he needs no help for himself but is prepared to talk to the therapist about his sick companion. Moreover, he points out to the therapist more or less bluntly what kind and what degree of cure he wants for the patient. It often turns out that he principally wants his afflicted partner to be even more docile, more cheerfully obedient, to be made perfect, in fact, in the functions on which he, for his own relief, wants to rely even more than hitherto.

The therapeutic goal he formulates is often in grotesque contradiction to the actual sickness and to the appropriate cure expected by the patient himself. Here, for example, is a father with a badly inhibited, stuttering son. The son wants to be rid of his stuttering. Ostensibly, the father, too, wants the stuttering eliminated, but in a long conversation with the doctor he complains in the end much more about the fact that his son makes use of "ugly expressions," that he defies his father with "vulgar words," that he flares up too easily, and that once, completely out of control, he contradicted his father. It is perfectly clear that unconsciously the father does not want his son to have freer expression but wants him to express himself with more propriety. To put it another way, if the psychotherapeutic cure of the stuttering should lead to the son later using even uglier or more defiant words, then it would be better that he go on stuttering. In fact, it turns out that the son's neurotic speech defect is closely connected with an inhibited protest against his father's constant browbeating. How is the young man going to get rid of his stuttering unless he is first helped to express his accumulated, suppressed aggressions? And so the course of therapy described by the father is impossible. The father has to decide whether he wants to have an even more obedient son or a boy who does not stutter. Since, naturally, the psychotherapist considers only the second course justifiable, he must try to change the attitude of the father, who is obviously much more disturbed by his son's threatened rebellion than by the boy's ailment.

A similar problem occurs with a mother who brings in for consultation a son with neurotic mutism (dumbness). The son hardly speaks at all in school. Because he does not answer his teacher, he has failed to be promoted with his class. Yet he is quite intelligent. But he will not speak what he knows and in general will not talk at all when asked to. He talks spontaneously only during play or in some other altogether unthreatening situation in which speech is not demanded of him. This shows, of course, that his organs of speech are quite intact, but his education and future are seriously threatened on account of the mutism.

In this case, too, it turns out that the mother complains to the psychotherapist much less about her son's handicap than about his lack of discipline. Finally, she explicitly condemns him for bursting into the table conversation unasked, even in the presence of guests. And she says he is dreadfully egoistic and defiant. She produces endless proofs of his defiance. Thus it becomes clear that the ostensible lack of consideration and the defiance on the part of the boy are her real problems. She suffers much more from them than from his dumbness. The dumbness, moreover—as is established by a detailed psychoanalytical examination—is in fact the disguised defiance of an enormously sensitive and vulnerable youngster. It is the only way left to him to express his resistance. This defensive attitude was originally directed almost exclusively toward his mother—an unusually possessive, octopus-like, grasping woman. Later his defiance becomes generalized. Rebukes from his teachers, felt by him to be unjust, wound him so deeply that he immediately falls silent in their presence. He uses his mutism as defensive armor, simply cutting off contact with the outside. Of course he can let nothing out, but neither does he have to let in any painful irritations.

Thus, as in the previous case, the psychotherapist sees at once that the boy will speak very little as long as he is not given more freedom and as long as he is deterred by painful criticism. Here, too, one cannot confine oneself to the traditional attitude toward a parent if one wishes to institute a sensible therapeutic procedure. But how can one influence a tyrannical creature so lacking in insight, if as therapist one pursues diametrically opposed intentions?

One must devise a test of some kind to measure the willingness of the active, dominating family member to cooperate. It is helpful to listen quietly, without immediate protest, to his version of the patient's ailment, no matter how absurd his proposals for treatment may appear. It is good if the conversation can be managed so that the relative feels encouraged to express in full his grievances against the patient. However egocentric these grievances may appear, however unrelated to the actual neurosis of the patient, they deserve to be taken seriously. The father of the stutterer and the mother of the mute boy do not just pretend but actually do suffer from the disguised rebelliousness of their sons. They are really afraid that their sons might attack them or leave them in helpless isolation if granted liberty.

As soon as an exploitive relative of this sort begins to talk seriously about his own difficulties with the dependent patient, he automatically offers himself as a kind of patient too, that is, as a person who is suffering. He may offer the therapist some such intimation as this: "Look, I too am a person in great distress. Think what the patient is doing to me." Often, such recitals of the disappointing experiences with the patient sound like direct apologies, as with the father of the stutterer and the mother of the speechless boy. The relative knows subconsciously, of course, that it is he, from his exalted position, who has terrified the patient and made him sick. And he expects that the psychotherapist will quickly hit upon this connection. So he adopts the preventive tactic of making the patient out to be very bad and himself to be the unhappy victim, hoping thereby to exculpate himself morally in the eyes of the therapist. The accusatory denunciation of the patient is then really a preventive defense against an anticipated rebuke from the psychotherapist.

In any case, one must not interrupt the relative's complaints about his dependent partner, and on no account should one allow oneself to be provoked into turning the tables and vigorously defending the patient against his accuser. Only when the domineering party begins to realize that his version, too, is being taken seriously, that he is being looked upon as a suffering human being who has not fared well with his pretensions, only then has a step forward been taken. Not infrequently, the relative will then spontaneously begin telling his life story and talking about the many hardships to which he has been exposed since childhood. This—and it sometimes happens in the first conversation, though more frequently in later meetings—shows that the relative is trying to present himself as a fellow patient. He is descending—cautiously and hesitantly—from his pedestal as the imperious giver of commands or menacing potential opponent of the therapist and exposing himself and all his weaknesses. Of course, hysterical tactics may be at work here too; it may be a momentary, exhibitionistic gesture on which the therapist cannot yet rely too confidently. But one should react positively to such an offer, being careful not to force by too vigorous exploration of memory the self-revelation of the relative. His position in the family indicates that it would probably be too disturbing for him if he were to hit upon the idea that his role as normal family member was being undermined through a subtle interview technique. He must be given time to try out and then cross a bridge which at first must seem to him very unsafe.

There are relatives who in concurrent family therapy are successfully treated for months at a time along with their dependent "patient" without ever fully admitting that the sessions principally give them therapeutic relief. They begin every hour with a brief report, as though incidental, about the patient, and then get around to discussing some personal difficulty of their own. In reality, they work in these hours principally on their own neurotic problems, but out of anxiety they mask their treatment by pretending to be helpful relatives supporting the simultaneous treatment of the patient. Other relatives, after a few preparatory conversations, are able to assume fully and formally the role of fellow patients in the family therapy.

One factor is decisive for success in remaking an exploitive relative into an implicitly or explicitly cooperative fellow patient. He must recognize that he is having an easier time when he can deal with his problems by himself without being dependent on a servile family partner as whipping boy, scapegoat, paranoid companion-in-arms, supportive assistant-ego, or pliable substitute love object. After all, it costs him considerable effort to train the dependent family partner or partners for the special roles he has imposed on them to get rid of his tensions. The partners often show increasing resistance, and the road to the doctor is frequently a significant indication of the strength of that resistance. If the young stutterer and the neurotically mute schoolboy finally succeed in getting to see a psychotherapist, that is a first, though still very tentative, success in their subterranean struggle against parental oppression. And the relatives responsible also betray by their uneasiness that they see their rule over the neuroticized children threatened. As therapist, one can offer the exploitive family member, without having to call the largely unconscious processes by name, some such deal as this:

"You say you are ready to release your son from the prison of his role, which was devised purely to relieve you of your tensions. In return for that, I offer to support and strengthen you therapeutically to such a degree that you will be able to handle your problem on your own, without coercing assistance."

If one seriously tries this and does it discreetly, one will be able to win—sometimes to one's own amazement—even refractory relatives to a fair degree of cooperation in family therapy. But one must learn to accept that in other cases even strenuous and well-considered attempts fail to transform a family's disturber of the peace into a cooperative partner.

We have shown that family therapy is needed when an individual is involved with one or more partners in such a close, specific dependency relationship that he cannot take on his problem himself and work on it alone through individual treatment. The concept "specific dependency relationship" means that a kind of neurotic imprint has appeared. This indicates not only that the individual is dependent and in need of support but that on the basis of this condition he has become firmly attached to one particular member of the family. And so the partner is not simply exchangeable. And this as a rule presupposes that the specifically chosen partner has contributed a great deal on his side to the attachment that holds the two firmly together. Perhaps it was he who attracted to himself the need of the other member of the family to cling and now uses it for his own purposes. This would be the pattern of the case just described, in which the neurotic dependency need of one part of the family coincides with the active, neurotic, grasping tendency of the other part. This kind of symbiotic—or parasitic—combination of "victim" and "exploiter" can wreck an attempt at isolated individual therapy of the "victim" against his "exploiter," whereas family therapy, if it can be established, may lead to gratifying results (see case history in chapter 13).

Sometimes, what seems to be this sort of family configuration is only so when viewed from the outside. One finds in the family a particularly un-self-confident, dependent member, but no specific and no reciprocal dependency relationship has been formed. The person depends on one or more partners, yet no one has responded in a neurotic way to this need. Thus the dependency relationship is a one-sided configuration. This can be explained more easily by means of a concrete example.

A young woman has a cardiac neurosis with fits of anxiety and numerous peculiar neurotic fears. She is afraid to stay at home alone or go out alone to shop. Because of her anxieties, she is very modest in what she asks for, so as to keep her husband in a good humor and assure his continued, considerate protection. But her husband is perfectly well balanced and shows no tendency to exploit. He would never dream of blackmailing his wife through her weaknesses. She could be quite sure of him without having to make special masochistic sacrifices. And so the one-sided unspecific dependency relationship is dictated simply by her individual illness. There is only the appearance of a mutual marriage neurosis. In reality, the wife's illness is not dependent on a group conflict. This time the group problem—that is, the clinging of the wife to her husband—is only a secondary effect of her quite personal illness. In this marriage there has not been the slightest sign of an anxiety-neurotic character change such as was described in the last case.

Here, family therapy in the strict sense would not be indicated. The unspecific nature and the one-sidedness of the dependency make it more likely that this woman would be better helped in individual treatment. In her anxiety, she will be sure to transfer to the relationship with the doctor a considerable part of her need to cling, without thereby getting into an emotional dilemma or driving her husband into jealous opposition and setting up a tug-of-war for her person. The doctor, by suitable individual therapy, can make her gradually more self-confident and courageous. He can steer the transference so that the patient, in the course of the treatment relationship, learns at least partially to overcome her inner compulsion to passive submission.

In such cases, the separation of a patient from his closest partner through the choice of individual therapy can be very advantageous. Joint marriage therapy in the instance just cited would have the disadvantage that it would unnecessarily strengthen the phobic clinging of the wife through the very form of the treatment itself. Moreover, one finds in such purely one-sided dependency relationships in family therapy that as soon as the first symptoms of the real patient have improved there is scarcely enough material left for joint work. The healthy partner quite rightly feels that he is simply a bystander and his peripheral participation in the treatment would in part bore him and in part just prove painful. In this case, family-therapy treatment would be meaningless.

It is often useful, with the patient's permission, to orient his stable relatives in cases involving neurotic anxiety—at the beginning and also perhaps once during individual therapy. Patients with disturbances of this sort must learn during therapy to expose themselves gradually to greater and greater tests of courage, and it is important that all concerned—patient, doctor, and family—should understand this procedure.

It is very difficult and not especially rewarding to explore in detail the narrower criteria of objective indications of a need for family therapy. As has been mentioned, many different, quite ⁻istinct arrangements are possible. One makes altogether different demands of the participants in psychoanalytically oriented marriage therapy from those one makes, say, of the relatives of a schizophrenic boy whom one wants to bring together with the patient and, through a specific technique, leads into improving the blocked family communications system. Again, different standards must be considered if one is about to begin treatment of the counseling sort with a helpless family which may not be able to follow a strictly regulated routine, etc.

The question arises whether being from a particular social class may not be one of the positive or negative criteria of selection for psychotherapy and in particular for family therapy. In fact, it has been shown again and again that persons from the lower classes are less often selected for psychotherapy and in particular for family therapy. Sager and his New York family-therapy working group have divided 157 patients they examined into five classes, according to education, profession, and income.[82] They assert that those from the upper classes could be more easily persuaded to go into family therapy. Of those patients finally selected for family therapy, 89% of class 1, 75% of class 4, and only 60% of class 5 actually showed up together with their families for treatment. But even with the preliminary processing and selection by doctors, lower-class patients did worse; they were less often found suitable for family therapy. Although this work group says that they did not allow themselves to be influenced in the selection process by social prejudices, they may have found it easier to work with upper- and middle-class patients than with those from the lower classes.

However, findings of a quite different sort exist. I have directed for almost ten years a polyclinic for family therapy and counseling in the working-class quarter of a big city, and there to my amazement I found conditions especially favorable for family-therapy cooperation. The proportion of families ready to present their common problems openly and discuss seriously and intelligently the background of those problems was remarkably high. In fact, the impression was that with many workers' families therapy proceeded more successfully than with families in much better socio-economic circumstances. My observations and those of my fellow workers, discussed frequently in conference, can be summed up as follows:

1. In comparison with the numerous families we examined from the upper social classes, the conflicts in working-class families that brought them into consultation with a doctor seemed to us, on the average, especially genuine and important. It was our opinion that the reason for this was that interpersonal relationships in these families were closer and more direct; at all events, they were not so strongly blocked and deformed through complicated, narcissistic defense systems as with many patients from the privileged classes.

2. Because of the greater openness and less pronounced narcissistic incrustation in partner relationships, the therapist found it comparatively easy to establish a patient-doctor relationship quickly and clearly. If help was really desired by the family members, one had only to hit the right tone to be quickly accepted as trustworthy. And then the difficulties in communication, the problems of instinct, fear, guilt feelings in the background of the conflict were often revealed to a depth which otherwise is attained only after long reticence and much defensive maneuvering. This openness to the therapist inwardly and outwardly was often happily combined with a reliable capacity to persist in cooperation, sometimes through a number of years.

3. As a result of their positive attitude toward therapy, the workers' families treated in our polyclinic had a positive reflex effect on the motivation of the therapist (counter-transference). The feeling of accomplishment in family-therapy activity led a number of colleagues, despite the lack of recompense (the state authorized only one paid position), to take part for several years in the program of the clinic.

To be sure, the especially favorable results in Berlin-Wedding may be related to the particular characteristics of its people. Local character traits of the Berlin working population might account for the willingness and the capacity to cooperate on the part of these people, so the observations made here cannot by themselves serve as the basis for sociological generalization (compare also chapter 15). Nevertheless, there seems to be no incontestable support for the widely held belief that within the working class there are fewer objectively qualified candidates for family therapy or for various forms of psychoanalytical psychotherapy. In many places, persons from the lower classes are less often picked out for this kind of therapy or less often accepted for treatment and continue on with it; thus the situation is still unclear. The question has not been answered as to whether we are dealing with objective or subjective criteria, whether the difference is due to the patient or the doctor. Perhaps most psychotherapists are simply not equipped to address patients from the lower classes in proper fashion. Anyone who in his childhood and youth had little association with these social groups will have trouble as a therapist in inspiring real confidence in his approach and speech with these patients during the first interview.

Nobody knows in how many cases this lack on the part of the therapist has led patients to believe that he cannot help them with their problems. The language of psychoanalytical techniques approved by Freud in his treatment of upper-class patients and described in his case histories has contributed to the stereotyping of an analytical vocabulary for use with mature patients which surely is more suited than is generally assumed to better-educated patients. Certainly in psychoanalytical circles everywhere it is clear that for the best results one should address each patient in the way he understands best. Yet one finds, especially among young analysts, a widespread misunderstanding that the artificial, highly differentiated interpretations that they hear from their teachers constitute psychoanalysis in its purest and highest form and should be unconditionally striven for. Out of this misunderstanding comes the fear of approaching too closely patients who have little verbal dexterity and tend to describe inner processes too directly or coarsely. This is deprecated as "not sufficiently analytic." Of course, it contradicts Freud's prediction of fifty years ago that a simplification of treatment techniques would be necessary for psychoanalysts in public institutions, who would be dealing with patients from lower social levels. "We will have to seek out," so he advised, "the simplest and most easily understood expression of our theoretical teaching."[32]

When now and then in medical reports a patient or a family is described as not intelligent, discriminating, or cooperative enough, it is always possible that the doctor is simply unable to adapt to the communications level of those seeking advice. This raises the more general question of the qualifications the therapist should have in order to work successfully, especially in family therapy (see chapter 11).

A final comment about the relationship of socio-economic factors and the criteria for family therapy. Whether a neurotically disturbed family is able to obtain family therapy does not depend, of course, on whether they are suited for such treatment or are able to get help from a competent and willing therapist. Countries such as Germany which deal with sickness largely through a system of health insurance, have had, until now, severely limited family therapy. The relatively modern medical-payment system in our country is still oriented to the treatment of individual patients. Even in cases where for the cure of a psychically disturbed individual—a child, for instance—the joint treatment of a relative is essential, nothing is done to promote joint therapeutic treatment. According to established regulations, the relative can only get parallel treatment as an individual who is sick. The fact that many psychic illnesses in families—the following case histories will prove the point—can be cured only through the joint treatment of apparently healthy members has not yet been accepted by health-insurance agencies or by the overwhelmingly sociopolitical lawmakers. Thus, health-insurance agencies systematically block the possibility of fully utilizing the opportunities for family therapy among all segments of the population. At this time, only prosperous families can afford the luxury of family therapy on a private basis with an established therapist. Hitherto, there have been only educational counseling institutions (which often, because of overwork, can provide only advice); a few university clinics have also been in a position to offer this modern and promising type of treatment to less wealthy families. It will be one of the tasks of the urgently needed reform of the health-insurance system to correct this failure, and soon. At any rate, the day is not yet in sight when the prophesy uttered by Freud[32] a half century ago will finally be fulfilled: that the aroused conscience of society will open to the poor and the indigent unlimited access to appropriate methods for the application of psychoanalysis.

11

What Sort of Therapist Is Right for Family Therapy?

A married couple are hopelessly at odds. They come to see a therapist. The husband presents the problem in a lively and much too facile manner, and gives the impression that he is completely open to help from the therapist. He says he is confident he will receive this help and expresses his thanks for the opportunity of discussing the problem, even before he has had any help at all. His wife, on the contrary, remains withdrawn, as though she would like to see the attempt at therapy ended as quickly as possible for both herself and her husband. She obviously scents in the therapist a potential opponent and is trying to protect herself against his anticipated criticism. What is to be done with this case? According to established tradition, all one would have to do is ask oneself: Are these two people objectively suited for treatment or for counseling? One might have them tested initially by a psychologist, who could determine with greater authority the suitability of the pair for one method or the other. The question of their suitability for treatment would then be independent of the person of the therapist and would be simply a problem in objective psychological diagnostics. Among the questions to be answered would be whether each of the people seeking advice is sufficiently discriminating, intelligent, serious, altruistic, and cooperative, and whether they would be willing to examine and solve their marriage problems as a joint endeavor.

The purpose of these considerations is to determine the so-called objective indication. Are the couple suitable for therapy? Of course, it is all too easy to overlook the obverse question:

What about the suitability of the therapist for the patients? Has he the prerequisites to treat the problem successfully? In contraposition to the "objective indication" regarding the couple, how does the therapist rate in what might be called the "subjective indication"?

If this question seems startling at first glance, it is because of the traditional, authoritarian-tinged self-confidence of doctors, psychotherapists, and marriage counselors too. Members of these professions believe that because they are reputable practitioners who have passed examinations and may even have had didactic analysis, they are automatically competent and beyond this are obligated by their work to take into consideration objective criteria only. If, however, a therapist wants to try, for a change, to free himself from this traditional overvaluation typical of his profession, it may be useful for him to ask: Am I, as a therapist, suitable for these people in need of help? Do I feel myself in this specific case adequate to these clients? What effect does this married couple have on me? Can I work with the person who eagerly seeks my help, without becoming too close or developing an anxious defensiveness? Can I, on the other hand, turn toward the obdurate, stubborn partner without dismay but with friendliness and optimism? Have I within me a certain confidence that I can helpfully inject myself into the disturbed communication between these two people? The feelings registered within oneself deserve at least as much consideration as criteria as do personality tests of the clients, no matter how discriminating. However subtle the information these tests reveal about the applicants, they tell me nothing about whether I as a therapist can make successful contact with these people, so that meaningful help will result. If a therapist makes a practice of testing the feelings aroused in him during the first interview and examines them carefully as indicators, he will benefit considerably.

Moreover, it is undeniable that feelings of this sort play a role in decisions concerning treatment. How often does a therapist undertake a treatment that is objectively too difficult, simply because he allows himself to be misled by an unexamined sympathetic impulse. Or someone else puts an end to an objective, thoroughly promising therapy, simply because the patient awakens fear in him or offends his narcissism. So, if the therapist takes into account his feelings, consciously he is doing something new only insofar as he is acknowledging one of the determinants that has always influenced the situation, instead of merely negating it.

That a family therapist should examine his own mental and emotional attitude seems strange and disturbing only to those who are not accustomed to it. In reality, one can effectively reduce one's feelings of anxiety in this manner. Specifically, one can relieve oneself of an illusion that may be very troublesome. Many therapists, even analytically trained ones, seek through unwholesome perfectionism to make themselves in their therapeutic or counseling work mere agents or practitioners of a universally obligatory method. For them the supreme goal is to function as interchangeable operators of an objectively established, absolutely unambiguous procedure, as though every individual variation were only a disturbing factor to be eliminated as completely as possible. This perfectionism is easy to understand psychoanalytically and to forgive. Every therapist finds it hard to accept that he is unable to reduce to a desirable degree the psychic misery of all the people entrusted to his care. Experience demonstrates that fear of one's inadequacy increases the desire to cling to a protective and completely safe method. The more imperfect one feels oneself to be, the more perfect one feels one should be, in order to endure oneself. Even in the discussion of cases, one finds that the less good the group believes it is accomplishing in general, the more rigid and severe its criticism.

In the following case history, it will be seen that family

therapy entails a particularly heavy personal load for the therapist. And in fact the principal requirement for a therapist is an adequate emotional endurance capacity. If he desires in psychoanalytical fashion to open himself to all the wishes, fears, and aggressions of the various family members, he can endure this only if he himself is very well balanced and is positively motivated for this fatiguing task. Many older psychoanalysts deem it highly improbable that a therapist can be so constituted that he is able to analyze the mass of emotions and expectations in a neurotic family, without chaotic confusion or a drastic partisanship.[31] For this reason, they believe family therapy must necessarily bog down in crass generalities or turn into disguised individual therapy. That means the family therapist will, out of his own needs, secretly favor one part of the family and neglect another. They think that absolutely sovereign, nonpartisan, analytical family treatment exceeds the normal capacity of a therapist and is an unrealizable ideal.

Meanwhile, it has been proved by the many family-therapy working groups all over the world that family therapy in the psychoanalytical sense is practicable. The generalized objection rests on a prejudice, which ultimately amounts to an ideologizing of the Oedipus complex, although Freud nearly half a century ago declared that the working through of the Oedipus complex was the principal goal of psychoanalysis. In fact, it is extremely difficult, in a culture dominated by the rivalry principle as extensively as ours is, to escape the acting out of rivalry conflicts in the therapy of family groups. The tendency to defend the intimate union of two against a disturbing third must in family therapy be brought under control through a constantly renewed learning process on the part of the family members as well as the therapist.[78] But this problem, as is indicated by numerous successful treatments, is fundamentally solvable.

The defensive postulate that psychoanalytical family therapy will not necessarily come to grief because of the unavoidable inadequacy of the therapist (that is, his Oedipal fixation) does not in itself seem adequate. The reference to the enormous load of counter-transference for the family therapist remains important in that every prospective family therapist should give careful consideration to the question of his capability for this particularly difficult area in the application of psychoanalysis. He should try to determine whether his emotional predisposition corresponds to the pessimistic or the optimistic expectations of those assessing his potentialities in psychoanalytic family therapy.

To be sure, such a determination is not so easily made through simple introspection as through personal experience in didactic analysis, and, if possible, participation in a self-discovery group as part of one's psychotherapeutic education. In this process the motives will be more precisely sifted out that served as basis for the candidates' preference for this promising but difficult area of family therapy.

Some of these motives—the helpful ones and the questionable ones—will be briefly considered here:

The special interest in family therapy and its difficult problems may be related to the psychotherapist's own family roles. Has he seen in his own life the difficulty of trying to satisfy one's own narcissistic needs and at the same time help and cooperate with the other members of the family? Perhaps the therapist had a particular private problem in dealing with childish desires that conflict with the interests of his own family and in learning to develop "parental needs" with altruistic purposes, and through satisfaction of them to achieve compensation. For instance, to learn that one can give up bit by bit the pleasure of being cared for and praised, if in return, as a parent figure, one has the gratification of caring for and praising others? Bringing into balance the intra-individual and the domestic family relationships of childishly passive and maturely active needs, of taking and giving, might have been especially difficult for the psychotherapist in his own development, before he was able to achieve through his own experience the helpful insights that now reinforce his motivation to devote himself to family therapy. He sees the possibility of making his own painful but in the end successful learning process of use to others in family therapy.

Motivation of this type can certainly be more useful in a family therapist's work than the wish of more than a few therapists to compensate vicariously for unresolved conflicts in their own families by repairing other people's families. Many a therapist, for instance, would unquestionably like to educate a married pair or a set of parents to an attitude that he wished for in vain from his own parents. This can go so far that again and again he projects on other families his own problem and must try out on them solutions that are much more suitable to his own neurosis than to the conflicts of the families in treatment. Especially unwholesome would be the results of the wish to punish other parents vicariously for what one had to undergo oneself. Such a wish inevitably produces in the therapist an inclination to form a distrustful, prejudicial counter-transference against parents.

It is a highly questionable motive if a therapist is attracted to family therapy because he secretly hopes thereby to be able to work close to the surface. He feels no wish to touch on the deeper regressions to which one is inescapably exposed in individual psychoanalysis. This is a motive one encounters in young enthusiasts of group therapy. An inclination to a superficial kind of therapy is, however, hardly consistent with effective psychoanalytical family therapy. A family therapist so motivated runs the risk of neglecting the more profound elements in family conflicts in favor of superficial compromise solutions and specious conciliatory advice. There are instances, to be sure, in which even a simple, problematically oriented counseling technique can do some good. But in those cases where a thorough, psychoanalytically based procedure is called for, a therapist of this sort will, of necessity, fail.

Not easily distinguishable from the motive just discussed is the hope that family therapy will provide more attraction, more dynamism, more color than the usual long-term individual therapy. In family therapy, one will be less bored than in classical psychoanalysis. In many instances, it is the fear of the deeper unconscious processes that a not too stable therapist is warding against with this "boredom." He denies the enormously dynamic but also admittedly disquieting force of psychoanalysis. He reduces this uneasiness by withdrawing mentally from the patient, thereby achieving the transformation of his anxiety into a feeling of monotony. He is attracted to the more "colorful" family therapy because here he hopes for greater opportunities to unburden himself through action. He thinks he will not have to withstand such severe tension as in individual therapy as regressive configurations are slowly allowed to emerge. Here, too, the suitability of the therapist for work with families seems very questionable. Anyone unable to withstand the tensions of individual analysis without strong resistance will have even more trouble in enduring the complex transference and counter-transference difficulties in psychoanalytic family therapy.

The hope for special "colorfulness" in family therapy is also found in therapists with certain depressive traits; they promise themselves more active stimulation in the more mobile scenes of family therapy. Also, they recall that there are many instances of individual analytical therapy in which especially depressive episodes may be expected in the course of the treatment. They are afraid their own depressive traits may be activated in a disturbing manner. As a matter of fact, in family therapy a lighter "hysterical" note is more likely to enter in, because of the very nature of the arrangement. The agitated give-and-take of emotional interaction into which the therapist has to inject himself may have a desirable, stimulating effect on him.

To this extent, it need not be a drawback necessarily if the family therapist can make use of the special dynamics of family work for his own character structure. At the same time, it goes without saying that a family therapist must not have depressive symptoms in the clinical sense; otherwise, he could not inwardly gather up the multitude of problems in a complex family neurosis.

In this eventuality, disguised delusions of grandeur of the most varied kind may play a part as motivating factors. One man might picture himself as the powerful judge in family disputes. Another strives for the role of wonder-working samaritan with groups of the bankrupt and the desperate. Again, someone else may feel that as a family therapist he can outdo his psychotherapeutic colleagues in his daring.

Yet there is no denying the courage called for to burden oneself with the complex problems of a systematic family neurosis. And why should one not feel proud if one is able to summon up the courage to perform a meaningful, considered, well-thought-out, difficult task? A desire for omnipotence is disastrous only if it is acted upon blindly and without a reasonable appraisal of the risks. As, for example, if one embarks on a hopeless family analysis purely out of bravado and without adequate recognition of the limitations. Naturally, one must be ever conscious that thorough analytical work carried out on even a limited problem with a single patient is still much more valuable than family therapy that ends in chaos, however daring the arrangements.

Visions of greatness can also be satisfied in the thought that one is among pioneers opening up new, fruitful therapeutic terrain for psychoanalysis—and for society. Here, too, there is the question of how far ambition, rivalry, envy of Freud, etc., distort one's view of the realities or, the other way around, sharpen it usefully in certain areas. It can be said, in general, that those who experiment in a relatively new field can make good use of some trace of pioneer megalomania to withstand the expressions of disapproval and prejudice from the traditionalist camp.

Actually, many of the just-listed, more-or-less unconscious motives that may form a basis for a preference for family therapy are rather suspect—assuming such motives have not been subject to adequate review examination. Among the unwholesome motives (to summarize the matter) are, for example, the compulsion to diagnose families on the pattern of one's own family neuroses and to try to heal them accordingly, or to take retribution vicariously on the parents of others for the injustices suffered at the hands of one's own. Especially dangerous is the wish of some unstable psychotherapists to retreat into family therapy because, afraid of the unconscious, they hope most easily to find in family work an opportunity for active, superficial therapy. For aspirants of this type, family analysis would quickly break away from its vital connection with psychoanalysis and turn into wild, dilettante pragmatism.

It is, of course, to be expected that the major objective difficulties in family therapy are most likely to be disastrous for the person whose motivation as therapist is least suited to his task. The complex structure of family neuroses, with the various mutually supplementary and crisscrossing elements of conflict, demands cautious, precise work with the various participants. If the family begins to sense that the therapist's behavior toward it or toward one of the group is tinged with ambition, fear, desire for revenge, desire to seduce, the therapist pays for it. They play with him, they stage a tug-of-war, or they simply get rid of him. In families with symptom neuroses, he can easily be drawn into the inner family conflict. Neurotically disturbed families will unite to disarm him, misleading him, for example, and thereby paralyzing him, or they too may throw him out at once.

EXAMPLES OF FAMILY THERAPY

12

A Working-Class Family at War and at Peace

Here comes a young woman, pale and woebegone, and in a dull voice she complains of troubles with her husband, her father-in-law, and the father-in-law's mother. In the same breath she mentions her own headaches and stomach aches, and spontaneously volunteers the conviction that these physical ills are connected with her family problems.

Formerly she had been a nurse's aide in a hospital. Now, as the mother of two children, a son and a daughter, she is simply a housewife in a home owned by her father-in-law, who lives there with his mother. She is a fugitive from East Germany; all her relatives and childhood friends are far away.

Around her there are only her husband's acquaintances and his family, and she explains that everyone in the family is at odds with one another. The grandmother obviously still plays a domineering role. At the time of her marriage the young woman believed that she had found a husband especially in need of and dependent on her love. He had lost his mother early, and it seemed to her, since she too was lonely, that they were very necessary to each other and because of that their bonds of affection would be strong. But: "For a long time now he has hardly spoken to me at all. Not a single blessed word. As for our son, he simply swears at the boy. I can't stand it any longer." Since he has become so harsh and strict, she has lost all physical affection for him and feels only repugnance.

The young woman is visibly crushed and helpless. She weeps while telling her story. But she is a sensible person with intelligent ideas and is trying to understand why her husband torments her so by his behavior: since childhood, so she reports, he has known nothing but hatred and quarreling. His parents had not had a good relationship with each other. Now his grandmother hates his father, his father hates his grandmother, but both are united in tormenting her husband and herself. And the grandmother is beginning to stir up trouble among the woman's children. "I believe that in this family harshness and hatred are handed on from one generation to the next," she says. She sees it all clearly. She sees, too, that her husband might behave differently toward her if he did not have to put up with so many insults from his father and grandmother. But she just can't bear it.

The doctor proposes that she bring her husband with her to the next session. "But he will not say a word," she objects. Nevertheless, she will try to arrange the meeting.

And, in fact, the husband does appear at the next session. The therapist first speaks alone with the sullen, withdrawn, taciturn mechanic, a bearlike, muscular man. He talks awkwardly, but it is apparent that he does not really want to express what's on his mind. Everything he says sounds like a growl. Obviously, he expects to be reproached and to be asked to be gentler toward his wife. In any case, he is prepared for self-defense. Gradually, his wariness relaxes and brokenly he reveals something of himself. "My wife always insists that I should speak up and say what's what, but often I say something different; otherwise, I wouldn't get anything at all from Granny and my father." And slowly he comes out with the fact that no word of praise has ever been said to him at home. He has to put up with all kinds of things from his father and Granny because he and his family live in his father's house and don't pay rent. He has spent so much time on repairs to the house that he has no outside interests or companions whatever.

He takes a piece of paper from the doctor's desk and sketches all the things he has changed and renovated on the farmstead. He draws and draws, very precisely, and keeps asking the doctor if he understands. The therapist then sees the light: now this man is gaining confidence. Talking is not really his thing; working with his hands is. Now he is testing me to see whether I will acknowledge him by saying something favorable about his work. The doctor makes good this expectation. "So you do see," the man says, "and here my father said that all this work was nothing at all and a real carpenter could have done it better. When it came to fixing the barn door, he hired a carpenter for that. I was forbidden to do it. Just the same, I would probably have done a better job," etc., etc.

So it goes for half an hour, and the next visit is the same. He explains to the doctor a job he did for his company, with which they were unjustifiably dissatisfied; and all the while he makes drawings of an intricate placing of pipes. "They're the kind of people you can't do anything right for. They bombard me with words. I swallow it all, but finally I get mad even at the flies on the wall. That's how furious you can get."

He talks on and on. He is so oppressed by doubts about whether he is any good at all that he uses the opportunity to talk to the therapist principally for self-justification and reassurance. Like a small boy who has always been criticized and who for the first time meets someone who praises everything he paints or makes with his toolbox. He gains assurance through an almost wordless contact, for the doctor says little except to murmur his understanding. How can this man learn to be good to his wife so long as he does not seem to himself to be any good, and always feels like some kind of a culprit? Grandmother and father obviously know all too well how to make him feel guilty. In his awkward, tongue-tied way, he is restive, frantic. And he knows only one way to preserve some small self-regard and continue to seek favor: to work with his hands. But even in this he gets nowhere. No matter what he does in the household, it's as though he were jinxed. He is diligent, yes, more than that. "I can't take any time off at all." By this he means that he cannot bring himself to stay away from work the way his companions do, because of a cold or some minor ailment. "There is noth-

ing worse for me than Sundays and holidays." Nor does he like
to sit at the table and talk things over with his wife. "But she
probably would like that, she is used to it from her own family,"
he says.

There he is quite right. His wife is in need of friendly conversation, affectionate concern. She likes to think and needs some
kind of intellectual exchange. Instead, she is isolated in a strange
family in which people habitually attack one another or defend
themselves. And her husband passes on to her and the children
much of the pressure exerted on him by his grandmother and
father through their constant complaints and quibbles. To make
up for his sullen moods and show his wife his love, on Sundays
he makes furniture or other useful objects for her and is amazed
that she shows no appreciation or gratitude. This is the source of
a tragic misunderstanding: he believes he has only to make
more and better things and then people will be satisfied with
him. His wife, of course, does not want him to work more but
to talk with her more. Meanwhile, the more downcast she becomes and the more she voices her disappointment, the less he
talks. Or if he speaks at all, it is only in a sullen growl. That is
his family's way, the only way he knows: expect blows and hand
them out. If someone disapproves of you, torment him all the
more.

The preliminary diagnosis is that the woman is less disturbed
than her husband, although it is she who developed physical
symptoms of illness under pressure of tension and he would
never have thought of seeking help from the outside. He reacts
to his feelings of guilt and rage with defiant silence or cursing.
His psychological defense mechanisms, his verbal inadequacy
and clumsiness, could easily lead one to consider him hopeless
for intensive therapeutic work, and to offer further treatment
to his much more approachable wife, who wants to express
herself. Actually, in the husband's case, the doctor is a little
afraid that he may not be able to understand him well enough
in the definition of his problem, with only the aid of the technical drawings and descriptions of his work. The man must
gradually learn to feel that his world is one in which the
therapist can find his way; that the doctor, when he expresses

appreciation, really understands what's involved—for example, the laying of the pipes—and is able to judge the drawings. The therapist believes that this man is not seeking meaningless compliments like alms, but a genuine, competent appraisal of his achievements, through which he is struggling to regain his self-regard. The doctor sees that he must take exceptional pains to be accepted by the workman as an adequate partner. And he decides to accept the challenge, because the husband is a key figure in the fate of the marriage and the education of the children. The therapist lets himself be swayed by his desire to help this sullen, angry man out of his deep narcissistic injuries. He hopes that then the man will show more of his already perceptible positive attitude toward wife and children. The therapist is less concerned about his chances of success with the wife. He feels that she is definitely motivated to modify, with his help, her defensive attitude toward her husband if the husband will only be a little more open with her.

The doctor has a few conversations with the man and the wife separately, and in between, all three talk together. It becomes fairly clear that grandmother and father are so hardened in their attitude that it is hopeless to bring them into therapy as well. These two have become habituated to discharging periodically their strong mutual tension by making the young husband a whipping boy. Obviously the treatment can strive only to shield the young married couple from the pressure of their elders and to put an end to what the young wife strikingly described as the family tradition; namely, the handing down of hatred and guilt feelings from one to another and from one generation to the next.

The therapist is accepted by both marriage partners, no doubt because he is able immediately to offer each what they had hitherto lacked. The young wife, isolated in the family, can finally express her problems and feel that she is understood; and the awkward husband, who first of all is seeking the restoration of his self-respect through praise for what he makes with his hands—he, too, attains his goal. The doctor gladly allows him for hours at a time to make drawings of his work and his plans for future improvements and decorations. The therapist understands clearly that this man cannot be a responsible husband and father as long as he feels himself a youngster who can do nothing to anyone's satisfaction. He has been showing his plans and executing his handiwork and has always failed to arouse any interest or get any appreciation for them. Therefore, let the treatment in this case follow the way many young people are handled—with them, psychotherapy just takes its course; thus the man will get the best help at once. You could say that the man was participating with the doctor in a rite of initiation that he had never before experienced. The doctor represents a father, who examines him severely and then accepts him: "You have done so well that you now have the right to be an adult." The young husband is working through his many scruples and self-doubts to prove that he does have this right of manhood. Only then will he trust himself to hold his ground against father and grandmother and to protect himself from their continuing humiliations. Because he was brought up without patient understanding or even a shadow of affection, he has been buried in moral self-denigration. It is necessary for the therapist to enter into the patient's doubts and bring his prolonged struggle for self-justification to a successful outcome. Otherwise, the young man would not willingly participate in the treatment.

After only a short time, a change is evident that in family treatment can always be regarded as a step forward. The young woman and her husband talk less about what the others have done to them, particularly what each partner has done that is not right. They talk almost exclusively about their own mistakes. In the first interview the woman had said: "Because my husband has so little love for me, I can't feel any physical affection for him." That means: He is responsible for my frigidity. The frigidity is only a natural reaction to his inconsiderate manner. After a few sessions she says: "I'm sorry that when it comes to sex I cannot give my husband what he needs. He certainly is suffering because of that." That shows that her purely defensive attitude is yielding to a more affectionate one. She wants to give him more now because she is grateful for the way he has changed.

She can scarcely comprehend it. It is so fine that her husband comes for these sessions. In recent weeks he has talked to her more than in the entire year past. He is more patient with the children, too. She makes excuses, apologizes for having represented him as so bad at first: "I am really ashamed of myself for that."

The husband not only becomes freer with her, he defends himself much more stoutly in his trade, where people have been used to his accepting all criticism without a word. Proudly he relates how his boss, a man the same age as he, had bawled him out because the laying of the pipes had not been finished yet. "I certainly showed him!" He had been able to prove to his boss that the drawings given to him were incorrect and for that reason certain parts of the job were impossible to do. The boss had to swallow the lecture because he was wrong and had no way to answer.

Even with the grandmother, the young man has succeeded in gaining the upper hand. As so often before, the old woman had said to him: "If I die soon, you will be responsible." He replied: "If I am responsible anyway, you can die whenever you like. As it is, you never stop talking about it."

Since then the grandmother has left him in peace. She gets out of his way when she sees him coming.

The therapist also talks to both husband and wife about their sexual difficulties. The wife is very much relieved by the husband's admission that he feels no injury or suffering as a result of her frigidity. Since he has noticed that her sexual reactions are closely tied to the ups and downs in the family tensions, he sees the possibility of making more of a contribution toward overcoming these difficulties in the future.

She is grateful for his understanding, and one way she acknowledges it is by an astonishing change in her appearance. After a few weeks, the once forlorn, shabbily dressed woman is hardly recognizable. She wears a youthful, modern hairdo and is stylishly and attractively dressed. Out of a prematurely aged, unattractive person has emerged a very pretty young woman who wants to woo her husband and no longer rejects him in disappointment. She has also understood that it would be overtaxing him to expect him so soon to provide a complete fulfillment of her need for an exchange of ideas, for stimulating conversation. For this, she knows she must find other contacts, which previously she had been afraid to seek.

Finally, even the problem of the couple's dependent role as guests in the paternal house will soon be solved. The husband speaks to his father about the matter, and the father seems ready to transfer the house to the son by way of a division of property. The son feels enormously encouraged by the prospect, especially since he will then have a stronger position with regard to the grandmother, who will still be living in the house.

This happens again and again in such treatment. If one person learns to feel more adult than before, he usually soon manages to change his circumstances accordingly. Then you see that the person was kept down because those around him noticed that he was unable to assert himself like a grownup. Now the young man feels stronger and is able to command respect from the domineering grandmother, the father, and the boss. And immediately he has greater strength to offer his wife and children, something that as a tormented, unsatisfied youngster he did not have to give.

As if by coincidence, the young wife's pains soon disappear completely. They have fulfilled their function, to mobilize help in a problem whose trail had to be followed rather far afield before the physical symptoms could be treated at their source. After three months, the couple feel that they are getting on well together now and can go on their own, without further help.

For a favorable outcome in a case like this one, there must be a basic positive bond between the married pair. The two must be well disposed toward each other. Each offers the other something which at the moment the other does not want, and each wants something that is not being offered. The mutual failure or misunderstanding is not an excuse for a narcissistic withdrawal of the couple from each other, as it is in less hopeful cases. Both want to communicate. But each feels the lack, at the moment of need, of a suitable response from the other.

And each tries, through defiant insistence on his own wishes, to compel the other to yield, with disastrous results. The husband, like a little boy, wishes to be acknowledged for his manual work, which is the only form of expression he is able to give to his feelings of affection. But the wife feels frustrated rather than cherished if on Sunday he makes a chair for her, or a little chest. What she seeks is conversation and tenderness. So she denies him appreciation for the chair; he in turn is silent or growls more angrily than before. She, the more delicate one, in the end breaks down, and sets up a situation in which a therapist can help them end their meaningless conflict and learn once more to understand each other's language. It is also quite sensible that they stop seeing the doctor as soon as they are able to communicate again. After they have learned, by way of the substitute figure of the therapist, to relax and revise somewhat their once impatient, stubborn desires, they can once more express these desires in conversation with each other.

This case is particularly instructive in showing the significance and problems of the therapist's counter-transference in this kind of marriage treatment. The therapist could easily succumb to the temptation to pity the intelligent young woman for having become involved with this type of awkward and intellectually unresponsive man. A therapist could provide substantial satisfaction in the role of substitute partner who would take a deeper and more understanding interest in her problems than her husband does. And from there, it would be only a short step to devoting a little more attention and friendliness to her than to her husband. By doing that, one would be entering into a tacit alliance with the wife against the husband—despite the family-therapy arrangement. This would disturb the atmosphere of the treatment, without the therapist's necessarily having committed any overt indiscretion in his verbal intervention. The husband would undoubtedly detect the suppressed tinge of rival feeling in the therapist and would draw back. The wife for her part would turn toward the therapist with exaggerated expectations. To be sure, in the intensive transference satisfaction, she would perhaps also be sufficiently relieved to lose her symptoms temporarily. But this would happen at the cost of withdrawal from her husband. The husband would hardly respond with loving gestures toward her and the children. Given his relatively crude make-up, he would, on the contrary, soon be terrorizing the family again, with his customary whipping-boy defense tactics. And after the conclusion of the supportive contact with the therapist, at the latest, a renewed breakdown on the part of the wife would take place.

In such cases, where one member of the family behaves aggressively and one or more are overtaxed and driven to a breakdown, experience shows that it is especially difficult for a doctor to divide his therapeutic good will evenly on both sides. Yet, without this prerequisite, a promising family therapy is simply not possible. Therefore, the therapist must be consciously at pains to approach the active family member and through understanding of his difficulties overcome any antipathy or even moral disapproval of him. For example, in the case of the mechanic who at first seemed so unfriendly, it turned out on closer acquaintance that behind the façade of coarseness, bitterness, and unfriendliness was hidden a most unhappy man seeking recognition, a person to whom one could gladly devote one's attention therapeutically without a trace of revulsion.

In addition to the counter-transference via the therapist, this case illustrates another special situation that has been described in detail in chapter 10. It is obvious that through the family-therapy approach, one can bring in the person who plays the dominant role in the family neurosis but who would never go to the doctor of his own accord. The husband, of course, has no symptoms in the narrower medical sense. His obduracy, after all, is not a failing that medical science would consider within its province. The man discharges on his wife and children the tensions created by the father's and grandmother's pressure on him. Only by shifting the point of reference to a sociopsychological one can it be made evident that in her symptoms the wife is really expressing a sickness that her husband originally has a greater share of responsibility for than she herself. She is the chief symptom in this sick family. Therefore, it is quite legitimate to draw in the husband as a fellow patient in spite of his apparent "healthiness." He is one of a type of latent patient who customarily escapes medical treatment, although on these people rests the greater share of responsibility for the neuroses in their families. The much-to-be-hoped-for extension of family therapy would afford, for the first time, a chance to bring to treatment these unrecognized patients who are of such importance, from a sociomedical point of view, in providing the causal background for appropriate therapeutic measures.

13

A Thirty-Year-Old Daughter
Grows Up

A mother and daughter from a neighboring city come for consultation. From their outward appearance one would hardly believe they were related. The mother, widow of a post-office official, is a resolute, stout, self-assertive woman. Although handicapped by a leg injury—she walks with a cane and limps—she gives the impression of an outspoken, energetic, decisive person. Alongside her the daughter, formerly a doctor's assistant but for a number of years considered incapable of working, appears helpless and forlorn: a delicate, black-haired girl with doll-like features, whose age (thirty) seems as incredible as the fact that she has been married for seven years.

It turns out that the mother's sister has recommended this visit to the therapist because of a mysterious illness of the daughter's that has lasted for years. It is visibly distasteful to the mother when the doctor requests that he first be allowed to converse with the daughter alone. She, the mother, emphatically declares that the therapist must hear her at the same time. But the therapist insists, and it takes a great deal of self-control for her to leave the consultation room.

In the interview with the daughter, one is struck by the constant repetition of such phrases as: "My mother says I am . . ." "My mother says I ought to . . ." "My mother says I have to . . ." Thus she presents herself as though her symptoms, her feelings, and her opinions are only partly hers, as though her mother were equally responsible for what has happened and is happening to her. On many points she is obviously at odds with the mother. For example, it becomes clear that she considers herself sicker than her mother believes she is. She feels, too, that her mother dominates her, gives her too little freedom. But immediately after saying these things, she begs the therapist for heaven's sake not to mention her complaints to her mother, who would be angry and would later scold her severely. Moreover, the mother means well and is really very good to her. "I can get anything from her." Thus one realizes that the daughter, despite certain feelings of opposition, is completely dependent on the mother. Of course, she wishes the therapist would help her to fulfill certain wishes that her mother has hitherto frustrated. But she herself does not want to be involved in this game. She does not feel equal to an open argument with her mother. Her anxious but also somewhat coquettish fashion of offering the doctor a secret alliance is strikingly reminiscent of the guile of a little girl who tries, by allying with her father, to keep her mother in check without the mother detecting any direct opposition.

Even after this first quarter hour's conversation, one can surmise on the basis of psychoanalytic experience that this young woman must have had an indulgent and easily influenced father. In his company she must have learned the tactics she is now trying out on the therapist. But one doubts that the father was strong enough to afford her more than a private, tender understanding. The mother's mastery appears absolutely unbroken.

In the following interview, in fact, the mother talks about the daughter as though about a child who belongs wholly to her. With remarkably naïve self-assurance, she praises the thirty-year-old: "She has always been most obedient. Even today, she is easy to direct." She has promised the daughter to give the doctor a record of the illness because the girl is afraid she cannot explain it all properly.

Clearly, the mother feels herself an indispensable auxiliary-ego to her daughter. She is indicating to the therapist, obviously, that he must not treat the daughter without her or in defiance of her. She must be included as interpreter; otherwise, no profitable communication with the doctor can be established. She must fear that daughter and doctor might reach an understanding behind her back and at her expense. Her parting warning to the doctor is that he not try to gain control of the daughter through exclusive, severe treatment: "Ever since the dentist used the drill once, she has refused to go back to him. She will not tolerate any compulsion, one cannot demand anything from her." That means something like this: "Don't you as a psychotherapist bore too deeply; otherwise, the treatment will be broken off immediately."

As for the sickness itself, for almost seven years the patient has gone through a long series of out-patient and hospital treatments. It began with headaches, dizziness, difficulty in breathing, fear of smothering, palpitations of the heart. The physical symptoms became chronic and were increasingly treated as hypochondriac. The girl gave up her work as a medical assistant, for years has not felt able even to do housework, and spends half the day in bed. She does not even pull herself together enough to give the mother a minimum of help with the household. She has undergone four fairly lengthy stays in various neurological clinics, including electro-shock therapy; a year of analytical psychotherapy; treatment by hypnosis; out-patient psychiatric treatment with a battery of psychochemicals; internal treatment with thyroid extract; diet, and so on.

The list of diagnoses is as varied as the catalogue of unsuccessful treatments: hyperfunction of the thyroid; hysterical neurosis; psychopathic personality with infantile hysterical traits; atypical depression. Several times the psychiatrists expressed a suspicion of creeping hebephrenia (schizophrenia). From the records it becomes evident that the mother repeatedly and rudely disturbed the attempts at medical treatment. Here, for example, are doctors' notes taken from a hospital record: "The referent (the girl's mother) is a highly intrusive woman . . ." "She sits all day beside her daughter and fusses over her as though she were a little child . . ." "Insists again and again that one must be kind to her daughter and must never treat her severely . . ." "The mother cannot be induced to leave the ward . . ." "This lady is completely lacking in insight although she pretends to understand everything . . ." "She has to be begged to shorten her visits a little . . ." "Keeps insisting that her presence is indispensable for the cure of her daughter." This treatment was, as a matter of fact, broken off by the patient and her mother. In the record of another useless hospital treatment, the conclusion is: "If any promising treatment is possible, it can only be resident psychotherapy . . . with protection from continued contact with relatives."

In short, so it seems, all treatments came to nought because of the mother's interference, because her opposition continued uppermost in every medical effort. Unsuccessful attempts had been made to protect the daughter from the mother, who, it had been assumed quite correctly, wished to keep the daughter ill, for some unconscious reason. But it is clear from the reports that, for the most part, the mother was regarded simply as a troublesome meddler, someone who had to be kept out of the treatment.

It is typical of traditional medical practice that again and again, without reflection, the old principle derived from organic medicine was applied. If an individual is sick, then he must be protected from harmful outside influences. Certainly this mother, as will be clearly demonstrated in what follows, might be counted as a "harmful outside influence." Yet the attempt forcibly to separate mother and daughter does not seem wise. The principle of organic medicine which holds that cure is possible only through protective isolation cannot be arbitrarily applied in a case of this type.

The daughter, although thirty, is in the psychic realm still in a symbiotic dependency on the mother. One might say that— psychologically speaking—she is still living as an embryo whose breathing center has not yet begun to function and who therefore needs the blood supplied through the mother's umbilical cord not to suffocate. Therefore, one has to stimulate the breathing center of this embryo into independent activity before one cuts the umbilical cord—not the other way around. Yet it was precisely the reverse direction that had been tried repeatedly in the young woman's medical treatment. They had tried again and again to make her reduce her contact with her mother or even entirely give up associating with her for a time. She had been told plainly: "We cannot help you if you continue to listen to your mother instead of standing on your own feet. You will simply have to free yourself from your mother." And in doing this, they had overlooked how severely they were taxing the patient. The more rigorous their insistence on her separation from her mother, the greater the girl's fear of being trapped in a helpless, completely unviable situation. And out of this dread she emerges each time with a compulsion to seek refuge with her mother, thereby defeating her doctors and receiving the support of her mother, whose motives for maintaining the symbiosis with her daughter still, of course, require elucidation.

The irritated reaction of the doctors shows that less attention had been paid to understanding the psychological background of this abnormally close symbiosis than to breaking it up. Such procedure leads to the conclusion that the doctors were simply enraged at the strength of the mother-child alliance, against which they could make no headway.

Now a possible alternative to treating the daughter separately in the face of the mother's opposition is the treatment of them together. But this means that one must turn one's attention to the mother with a friendly willingness to understand, for if one judges her secretly as a ruthless oppressor, no kind of positive therapeutic contact may be established.

Yet the mother seems just as *afraid* of letting go of the daughter as the daughter is of claiming her freedom. It is not clear what has caused this fear in the otherwise quite domineering mother. But one must assume this feeling in her, and then it immediately becomes doubtful whether the daughter's dependency automatically requires a more determined therapeutic approach than the mother's overprotective behavior. Is it not mandatory to regard both women as an entity in which the reciprocal involvement is so deep that it is difficult to know in advance how profoundly each participates in the motivation of the other? At any rate, it is helpful for the therapist to take the medical reports of the previous seven years as a chain of intimations that the physical symptoms are not the personal concern of the daughter alone but are related to the group neurosis.

At the same time, the question of the husband crops up. How is it that mother and daughter hardly ever mention the young woman's husband and he is practically never referred to in the numerous medical reports of recent years? Undoubtedly, this is a further indication of the exclusive clinging together of mother and daughter, but the question remains: What is the situation of this man, whose role the two women have obviously been able to undermine? If he is completely unimportant in the household, how can he put up with it? Or is his background position by no means as lowly as it seems in the make-up of the family neurosis?

The therapist regards it as his most pressing job to discover in a series of sessions with the mother why this seemingly energetic woman needs to cling so tenaciously to her daughter. The facts are soon uncovered.

This simple, apparently rather coarse-grained woman has had since childhood a deep-rooted problem with her sister. The doctor is told that the sister has always been especially dainty and delicate. "And she was always smarter than me." "She had no trouble getting mathematics into her head. She was very proud too, I am a much simpler person." "She can play several instruments, I was always good only at housework." "She was very spoiled, especially by our father." The sister, it turns out, has quite a different attitude toward life. She wears make-up, dresses in the latest fashion, is energetic and sociable, and through her marriage to an important businessman has attained a high social level, while the sick girl's mother has remained in the old milieu.

But in one respect the mother has always had the upper hand. This is how she reports it: "My sister was always weak and sickly. She couldn't stand up to anything. She often had to have special food, I ate my pea soup." "She would burst into tears at anything. I often felt sorry for her. Even when she took food on the sly, it was *I* who took the blame for it." "I always tried to protect her. Even in kindergarten, I always had her by the hand and I would say to her: 'Now come along carefully behind me and don't fall!' "

Without being aware of it, the mother assigns the same attributes to the sick daughter as she does to the sister. The daughter, too, has always been dainty, very talented, and brilliant at mathematics. She, too, is finicky about eating and has needed special foods. Also, she has been delicate and sickly all her life. Even the parallel of paternal pampering is not lacking. The father, who died during the daughter's puberty, had carried her to bed every night. He had been "infatuated" with her and couldn't refuse her anything. "With me, there was no such thing," she adds. She emphasizes what a good man her late husband was. But she mentions casually that he was "a little weak" and that she had to look after a lot of things that would have been distasteful to him.

There emerges very clearly out of this first assessment, which further evidence confirms, the problem that binds this woman to her daughter. She is experiencing with her a replay of decades of sibling rivalry. It isn't enough that in her childhood she had to live alongside a prettier, more refined sister who was her father's favorite and her own superior in almost everything. She has had to go through it all once more with her daughter, who outwardly and inwardly resembles the sister much more than she resembles the mother. As if in confirmation of this, the sister has on several occasions remarked to the daughter: "You would have suited me much better than you do your mother!" But, as with the sister, the mother has one way to make up for her feelings of jealousy and envy through a specific satisfaction: the daughter, too, is frail and sickly. And so the mother finds—just as she had earlier with the delicate sister—an excuse to use her greater vitality and strength to exert domineering overprotection. Is this the key to an understanding of the symbiotic mother-daughter neurosis? Is it possible that for the mother the daughter has to be sickly and dependent, so the mother won't hate her as a dangerous rival? And so the mother won't have to hate herself because of her own unworthiness, as might be the case if she were separated from the more favored, talented daughter?

It appears quite plausible that for the mother the daughter must remain a weak little creature who has to be held by the hand and who can be overprotectively ordered about. One is reminded of the words: "Come along carefully behind me and don't fall!" But they doubtless mean: "I will protect you as long as you walk behind me carefully, but I will let you fall if you should let go of my guiding hand and try to free yourself from me. I could not bear to see you triumphantly surpassing me the way my sister did."

Now one can understand very well when the mother reports in detail and with great pride how she has successfully suppressed her daughter's sexuality. Obviously, she has made use of every opportunity to inspire fear and a reaction formation against sexual desires. She praises her daughter because as a child she did not like to go to the beach, because the sight of "naked people" was repugnant to her. She had been irked by the many women in short bathing suits. The mother asserts that she had again and again warned the child against "wicked men." She made it a point never to leave the girl alone on the street and would admonish her: "Don't let anyone tempt you with chocolates, they'll make off with you!"

The mother also volunteers that the daughter had broken off an unsuccessful, year-long psychotherapy principally because the therapist had talked to her so much about sexuality.

Clearly, the mother is in this way giving a similar warning to the new therapist. In her seemingly quite factual statement there lies an unmistakable appeal: Now you realize that neither I nor my daughter desires that you should make her sexuality, suppressed with so much effort, a subject for treatment. If you attempt that, we will break off the therapy with you exactly as we did with the earlier doctor.

Throughout, one feels the mother's deep hatred of sexuality. And the question arises: How can this woman play watchman over the daughter's sexuality in this manner, since the daughter is thirty and has been married for seven years? Does she simply deny to herself the existence of the daughter's sexual life, or has it completely atrophied?

Conversations with the daughter and the mother gradually

give a clear picture of the remarkable origin of the girl's illness seven years earlier. At that time the daughter had met her husband, a thin, pale young man, an engineer. He was an only child, the spoiled son of a bus driver, and had just started on his first job, a very modestly paid one. As socially uncertain as the daughter, he, like her, had never before had any close friendship. The two young people were soon spending all their free time together. They grew dependent on each other and each seemed especially concerned not to be abandoned by the other. Then marriage plans were mentioned. The mother asserts that she was always against the marriage. She had often told the daughter that she was too young for marriage, that the man was not important enough and, besides, did not make enough money. But the daughter had not listened and had had her way.

Many factors, however, put in doubt the accuracy of this version. One can hardly believe that the daughter would ever have had the courage to oppose a determined protest by her mother. It is more likely that the mother—whose control over the daughter, of course, would have seemed threatened by the marriage—was not too unhappy with the choice of the timid engineer. Be that as it may, she arranged for the newly married pair to take up residence in her small house, and they had lived there for the seven years of their marriage. The young man at first gave in completely to the will of his mother-in-law, especially since she drew him into her overprotective care too. She exerted herself mightily to satisfy the various wants of the young couple—with only one exception: she was unsparing in her pointed expressions of horror over "dirty sex." And she arranged it so that in the house the young people felt constantly under her eye. They slept in the bedroom next to hers. The daughter was never free from the thought that the mother could hear everything from next door. And on many mornings the mother actually came out with certain insinuations: the daughter was looking poorly. She probably didn't get enough sleep. She should be careful not to overexert herself. Each time the daughter had believed that her mother's comments referred to sounds of sexual intercourse overheard during the night.

As a matter of fact, in the new marriage anything but an

active sex life prevailed. The inexperienced husband was awkward in his approach. Apparently quite unsure of his potency, he was unable to overcome the neurotic sexual fears that had been instilled into his wife. And the surmised supervision from next door helped dampen the originally enthusiastic but unsatisfying sexual activities of the young couple. Finally the wife bluntly rejected further sexual advances on the part of the husband. The husband, irritated by repeated failures of potency, obediently withdrew. From then on, the pair lived like good children, brother and sister, in the house of the mother, who seemed in no way unhappy about the asexual course of the daughter's marriage, whatever else she might reproach the young people with. When the daughter let it be known to the mother that nothing of an intimate nature was occurring between her and her husband, the mother—so the daughter reported—received the news without comment but with an air of satisfaction.

And so, at this point, the young wife fell ill. As it became clear in later psychoanalytical conversations, her headaches undoubtedly could be explained to some extent as hysterical conversion symptoms in direct connection with the unsolved problem. The chronic situation of temptation in the shared bedroom, combined with continual suppression of sexual excitement, led to tensions that found expression in various ways, including headaches, feelings of heaviness, and a fear of smothering. But one would certainly have no more than half understood the young woman's illness if one explained it simply on the basis of conversion hysteria stemming from internal sexual conflict. The question remains: What does the illness mean in the context of the dialogue with the mother? What is the daughter trying to tell the mother through her ailments, and to what extent does the mother comprehend the message? And finally, what does the illness mean within the triangle of roles—patient, mother, husband?

In family therapy (the concurrent type), the following answer emerges: mother and daughter have found in the illness a labile and by no means unthreatened compromise, which nevertheless has proved effective for years. Each derives from the situation some satisfaction and must at the same time pay a price. The daughter fulfills an unconscious wish of the mother's when as an ill, weak creature she clings to the "guiding hand" and walks "behind her." At the same time, she assuages the mother's fear of rivalry by denying her own sexuality and contenting herself with a mock marriage. In return for this, she worries her mother and arranges for herself a regressive substitute satisfaction by allowing herself to be waited on from morning till night and by leaving to the mother all the activities and responsibilities of running the household. She lies in bed for hours during the day, whines about her symptoms, reads popular magazines, and watches television. Marketing, cooking, washing, looking after the house are the mother's responsibilities alone. If occasionally the daughter goes through the motions of helping out, she immediately reports a worsening of her headache or other symptoms and lands right back on the sofa, a pathetic invalid.

If one wanted to state briefly the tacit agreement between daughter and mother, the text of the treaty might—from the daughter's point of view—read like this: I will sacrifice my sexuality to you so that your envy and jealousy conflict won't drive you mad. But in return I will remain a passive child who has to be cared for and spoiled and who leaves all the work to you.

Until now, both have kept this unconsciously executed contract. The daughter has given up the sexual side of her marriage, and the mother patiently takes care of and slaves for her extortionate child. The magnitude of her contribution is understandable only if one realizes that, though the work is drudgery, it fills her with pride. This was the narrow area in which she could always triumph: to withstand more than her sister (and daughter), to assume more responsibility in the day-to-day struggle for existence, to intercept the blows from the surrounding world, to eat simple foods, and so forth. These things she is accustomed to; they feed her ego and protect her against feelings of jealousy and inferiority. In her consciousness of unchallenged power over her daughter, she can even enjoy without ambivalence the daughter's advantages and exploit her in the role of "substitute for the ideal self." The qualities she does not herself possess—attractiveness, delicacy, cleverness—she acquires from her daughter by secretly fantasizing the girl as an extension, a piece, of herself. She can even participate in the daughter's relationship with her husband, though these relations, of course, must be supervised and desexualized in order that she not become, after all, the victim of her feelings of jealousy that have been suppressed with so much effort.

The therapist now understands why the mother is so afraid that he may bore too deep, that he may even eventually awaken the suppressed sexuality in the daughter and thereby embark on a successful therapy at the mother's expense. But if the compromise between the two has hitherto functioned so well, what can have brought them to the doctor now? After all, mother and daughter know from the many unsuccessful treatments that every therapist tries to attack the morbid arrangement in the family. What motive is at work now if the family, of its own free will, once more risks endangering the secret treaty? One must assume that the neurotic compromise is no longer fulfilling its purpose as well as in the past. In the course of the treatment it will be seen that two circumstances have led mother and daughter to try to find a better solution to their conflict.

After seven years of housekeeping and overindulgent care of the young people, and not least because of the enormous effort required to maintain her intimidating regime, the aging, partially crippled mother is beginning to be exhausted. Her weariness shows her that with the passage of time she is paying more in this business than she is gaining. Irrationally, she dreams that the therapist may be able to make her daughter healthier and more active without touching on her dependence or her sexual troubles. In any case, the mother feels overburdened and wants a change in the situation.

From the daughter's point of view, the problem looks like this: she feels that she cannot much longer expect from her exhausted mother the recompense of unlimited pampering. She is terrified that one day she will find herself a completely dependent, helpless child, with no protecting mother at her beck and call.

There is still another circumstance that threatens the neurotic compromise peace of the family. The first insight into this comes from conversations with the young woman's husband.

More than a head taller than his delicate wife, the husband nevertheless makes a boyish and embarrassed impression; yet he is very guarded. One notices at once that he tries to enlist sympathy for all that he has had to put up with because of a chronically sick wife. He describes in detail everything that has been done for his wife and what sacrifices he has had to make. He cannot have sexual intercourse with her because she is afraid of it and he has to spare her. He cannot go out with her or travel. Besides, she depends more on her mother than on him: "Mother and daughter, there's a combination, as if they were welded together!" He can get nowhere in the face of this. He comes home only to watch television and to eat. It is getting harder and harder to endure his wife's endless complaints about her illnesses.

At this point, with the husband emphasizing so strongly how impossible the situation is for him, the therapist notices that he does not ask whether there is any chance of improvement. On the contrary, when the doctor indicates that the treatment may produce a change, the husband's eagerness to underscore the absolute hopelessness of the household situation increases, just as if he did not want so much as to think about the possibility of successful therapy. He seems interested only in a consensus that he, an innocent, upright man, is forced to endure martyrdom, for which his wife and her mother are responsible.

It emerges further from the reports of the two women that recently the husband has been spending less and less time at home and, contrary to his former practice, is showing less and less interest in the ups and downs of his wife's illness and in her arguments with her mother. The two women have already formed the suspicion that the husband has perhaps found some place or someone from whom he is deriving compensation for his domestic disappointments. His parents? Another woman?

This then is the second new element in the family situation. The first: mother and daughter fear that they will no longer be able to sustain their reciprocally exhausting relationship because of the mother's failing strength. The second: the husband seems no longer to be playing his accustomed part wholeheartedly. A change in the neurotic family configuration appears unavoidable one way or another. And that is why a therapist is especially needed now, because they are afraid that a change might result in catastrophic collapse. To be sure, this statement should be qualified: only mother and daughter are seeking help. The husband seems, rather, to be afraid that the wife may become well again. The two watchful women are presumably right in suspecting that he has found a refuge outside the home, and they are considering the possibility of his completely breaking away soon. If this happens, the mother, of course, would have the daughter entirely to herself and would be spared her jealous anxiety. But, on the other hand, there is the dread that she would then have to carry alone the burden of increased reparations which the daughter would exact for being cheated of a life of her own. There would be an end to the measure of relief the husband furnished by taking upon himself at least part of the passive wishes of the young wife.

Altogether, the pressure of suffering in the family has led mother and daughter, at least, to seek relief through active cooperation in family therapy.

Mother and daughter are treated in separate sessions. The husband, who at first acts completely disinterested, is later included. In the young woman's sessions, the mother always plays a part, for the daughter reports at home everything that happens in therapy, and the maternal attitudes, too, are promptly retailed at the sessions.

If this were individual therapy, by the way, the therapist might be angry at this domestic indiscretion on the part of his patient. It would be one of those cases in which it would do no good at all to forbid bringing others into the analytical dialogue. This young woman is in no position to hide anything whatever from her mother. A therapeutic ban on such indiscretions would lead at most to the opposite result: the daughter would continue to confide in her mother but would no longer admit doing so to the therapist. In the rivalry for power with the mother, the doctor would be defeated and would himself become the one imperfectly informed. And this would lead to the failure of the treatment—just as all attempts at individual therapy with this young woman have come to nought in the face of the overwhelming mother-daughter alliance.

At the start of the treatment, the mother is clearly afraid of the doctor in his role as rival for the daughter. But she quickly relaxes when it can be demonstrated to her that the problem of the daughter is by no means to be solved one-sidedly, at the mother's expense. Instead, she notices that her own problem, involved in her daughter's, is being taken with the same seriousness. It thus becomes easier for her to talk about herself. In fact, she becomes very communicative. Out of the distrustful and competitive relative, there emerges a confident fellow patient who exerts herself vigorously to be accepted and to find understanding.

As a result of this positive relationship, she becomes open to the idea that the daughter has inherited the problem which she, the mother, had earlier had with her sister. It is bluntly suggested to her that she may admire and be proud of the daughter because of her special intellectual and physical advantages. In this respect, she is in fact substituting them, actually with the daughter's help, for an essential part of her own identity without which she is afraid she could not endure herself.

As she comes to feel safer with the doctor, she can also divulge her fury at the daughter. For just as desperately as she needs her as a substitute for the fulfillment of her own ideals, just so desperately does she hate the daughter as a potential rival and most of all as a little extortionist. Naturally, she feels that the daughter is demanding an exorbitant price for submitting to maternal authority and for giving up the expression of her own sexuality. And there are sessions with the mother in which almost nothing is brought out except a flood of complaints about the daughter's indolence, about her constant peculiar wishes, her ingratitude, her ceaseless whining about her head, her throat, her heart, etc. And so the mother feels exploited by the daughter to the point of exhaustion. And in the course of weeks the therapist feels that on the mother's side a plea is being made to him: "Help me not to lose my daughter entirely. I will give her more freedom, because I now understand that in time I would go to pieces if I kept trying to pay the price I have been paying her to forgo rivalry and in exchange for her childlike obedience."

Through careful interpretation, the mother is brought to the point of considering a new and better answer for the conflict with the daughter that has been deadlocked for so many years. Now, during therapy, she experiments with giving the daughter more freedom. She achieves this after she has, in the course of several hours with the doctor, worked through a part of her old conflict with his sister. She has succeeded in this working-through simply because the doctor has not repeated the pattern set by her father and son-in-law and unintentionally sustained by most of the earlier doctors: that is, a one-sided, affectionate attention to her rival (sister, daughter) and a neglect of or even an attack upon her own person. She can even admit to her rage at the daughter without having to fear that the doctor will rebuke or dismiss her.

It is of course inwardly clear to her that she has hitherto not allowed the daughter to get well. She observes, too, that the doctor has come to understand her part in the daughter's illness. But she is helped by the very fact that the doctor does not wish to turn away from her for this reason but on the contrary admits to her that she cannot behave "reasonably" toward the daughter as long as she cannot trust herself to bear her own problem without involving the daughter. Supported by a good transference and strengthened by a certain liberating insight into the background of her fears, she finally of her own accord allows more free play in the daughter's treatment.

The daughter fills the first hours with endless accounts of her illnesses, which she describes in a childish, whimpering tone. Parallel with the growing openness of the mother, she tells more about domestic occurrences. Finally, she reports several emphatically sexual dreams: a gentleman whom she likes takes her to his room; at a wedding she is invited to dance; a man pursues her and threatens her with knife and gun, she feels that the weapons are not very hard but are made of plastic. Although she becomes very excited in the process, she confronts the therapist with her suppressed sexual needs. The self-reassurance in the last dream that the masculine member is perhaps not so murderously dangerous but is made of plastic indicates her ability to come to terms with the subject. Instantly, however, the mother appears on the scene and goes to work on the daughter at home: dreams are like bubbles, no good will come of it if the daughter sees a bride in her dreams, etc. We can see that here the mother still feels threatened and must try even in the interpretation of dreams to prevent any improvement in this direction. Nevertheless, the relationship of mother and daughter has meanwhile become strong enough for them to be able to discuss this ticklish subject.

The daughter can talk in detail about her married life. Then it emerges clearly that she is developing a readiness to venture into a sexual relationship. She says explicitly that she would be happy if her husband were to make advances. She reports her own unsuccessful attempts to arouse her husband sexually.

The husband reacts rather defensively to the wife's improvement. In conversation with the doctor, he clearly tries to deprecate the signs of stabilization in the wife and marshals all contrary indications that she continues to be extremely ill. Only much against his will does he accept an invitation from the doctor to attend a session of all three—that is, including the wife.

There a highly significant argument breaks out between the husband and wife. The wife complains that the husband still treats her as an invalid who has to stay home. In fact, she now feels strong enough to go out with him. He shouldn't go on ignoring her. Also, she is suffering because he shows her no tenderness. Nothing occurs to the husband by way of reply except an enumeration of his many acts of thoughtfulness during recent years. After all, it was she who did not want sexual intercourse. Finally he insists that as long as she is not completely well, she cannot demand that he behave toward her as he did earlier. After all, he has suffered so much and given up so much, while she, after a brief improvement, has always collapsed again. She must certainly be overestimating her improved condition now, and even the therapist perhaps tends to see things in too rosy a light.

The doctor recognizes that the husband is unwilling even to admit the improvement in the wife's condition, nor will he support it by encouraging her. It is noticeable, too, that the reawakened sexual willingness of the wife obviously does not correspond with the husband's own wishes but runs counter to them. The therapist, for his part, tells the two people that they must come to a decision together as to whether they really want to enter into a marriage in the full sense of the word or continue their childlike playing house together. The young woman's state of health makes this clarification absolutely imperative.

After this joint conversation, the young patient feels herself further strengthened. Her physical conversion symptoms begin to disappear. She seldom complains now during the treatment sessions. And she makes up her mind to look for a part-time position as a technical medical assistant to an established doctor. The mother approves of this plan. And in fact the daughter has a good offer as the result of an advertisement. After several years of inactivity, she applies herself zealously to books so as to be prepared for the job.

By this time it is no surprise that the husband tries to discourage and intimidate the wife all the more, the stronger she becomes. He can no longer rest content by letting her lie like an unnoticed object in the care of his mother-in-law but must accept her as a partner. This challenge compels him to reveal a secret that explains his seemingly paradoxical attitude.

For two years he has been having an affair with a wealthy, widowed business woman. Quickly coming to a decision, he moves in with her and begins divorce proceedings. Before this happens, however, there are a few unavoidably violent arguments between mother and daughter on one side and husband on the other. Yet the disclosure of the husband's long-suspected infidelity and his departure have the effect less of a catastrophe than of clearing the air.

It is obvious that the therapeutic activation of the young woman, accomplished with her mother's help, has forced the husband to confess his secretly long-contemplated action and to assume full responsibility for it. The other implication, however, must not be lost sight of: the patient and her mother have finally summoned up the courage to admit the falsity of the mock marriage and to provoke the husband to his confession. The therapy has brought each of the family members to realize that he or she must confront the problem and find a new way out, once the disappearing illness of the young woman can no longer conceal from her or her mother or husband their own conflicts and the necessity of making their own decisions.

The young woman begins her part-time job. At first she has some difficulties with the work, which she has not done for years. Her handling of the pipette, the determination of the shades of blood samples, and the counting of blood corpuscles result in some failures. Also, the tempo of her work at first leaves something to be desired. But she is ambitious enough to overcome these difficulties. And her employer treats her with great consideration during the early period, until her improved performance finally leaves no cause for criticism. After six months, the woman is given full-time employment.

Three years later—the divorce has long since become final—she becomes friendly with a civil servant. Soon there is an engagement. To her amazement and pleasure, she observes that she finds full satisfaction in the gradually developing sexual relations. The mother, to be sure, regards this new involvement of her daughter's not without skepticism. But she does nothing to obstruct it, this being made easier by the fact that the daughter's present partner substantially surpasses her former son-in-law in self-assurance and determination. The mother realizes fully that she would risk losing completely the already weakened contact with the daughter if she were to engage in a tug-of-war with the daughter's new partner. She prefers instead to associate herself with this union as a helpful benefactress, in order at least to stay in the game.

By this attitude the mother herself anticipates any suspicions about her complete approval of the results of the treatment. It might have been suggested that she helped so readily only because the resulting departure of the former husband opened the prospect for her once more to secure control over the daughter and eliminate masculine rivals. And so she agreed to an apparent cure for the daughter which brought about the removal of symptoms but instituted a renewed, undivided subjection of the daughter to the mother. This interpretation simply does not hold up. Further events prove that the mother is in fact able to grant her daughter more freedom than before and even to permit her a sexual relationship without falling back into the old hostile jealousy. The daughter marries her new man and emigrates with him to a country outside Europe. Also, the divorced husband remarries.

Other possible objections deserve more serious consideration. Wasn't the therapeutic success with the young woman achieved at the cost of breaking up the family unit? Didn't the doctor through his intervention cause or at least hasten the loss of part of the family? And isn't this due to some extent to the fact that —contrary to the principles laid down in the preceding chapter—the therapist cooperated more strongly with one segment of the family than with the other—indeed, at the expense of that other? Suppose he did help mother and daughter in their common problem—in the end, wasn't the role of "disturbing relative" simply transferred from the mother to the husband?

It must be frankly admitted that family therapy in all likelihood hastened the external dissolution of the marriage. This resulted from the treatment's having revealed a hitherto obscured fact; namely, the already irreversible isolation of the husband from the family. Long before the beginning of the treatment, he had found a secret haven with a woman friend and had formed a lasting relationship with her. It was no longer possible, therefore, to motivate him to consider overcoming his difficulties within the existing marriage after all earlier attempts had failed. Nevertheless, it obviously would have been fine with him to go on leading his "double life" for a while. As things were, the formal, continued existence of the old marriage could be used by him as an excuse to keep from having to assume full responsibility for the new partnership. That decision caused him overmuch anxiety. Until then, he had been able to play safely the role of poor overgrown youngster, who could allow himself to be spoiled by his new friend, by his parents, but also in the house of his mother-in-law. Nowhere did he have to assume the full obligations of a mature man. In his marital household, all he had to do was sit at the abundant table of his mother-in-law and sympathize without obligation with his sick, childlike wife. He could accept the favors of his new partner without specific reciprocation as long as he could take advantage of his husbandly duties toward his sick wife as an excuse. That in reality he had never assumed the full responsibilities of a mature life companion and at the moment still did not trust himself to do so could remain his secret as long as his wife's illness continued and the emptiness of their relationship remained hidden. He could adopt only a defensive attitude toward therapy. For the therapist, there was no possibility any longer of helping to bridge the gulf between the young woman and her husband.

Moreover, it appears in retrospect that the role of the husband in the family neurosis was not as insignificant as one might have assumed at first from his passive behavior. He was not simply a pathetic fifth wheel but—at least in the end—actively contributed to the wife's chronic illness. Only as long as she was sick could he maintain the double existence that suited his passive wishes. Of necessity, he had to break away at the moment when he could not but accept her as a cured, mature woman with sexual demands of her own.

From this point of view, the therapy did not harm the husband either but, rather, brought him an important gain: it forced him to give up his slippery game, with all its burdensome self-deceptions and self-justified betrayals, and to make a mature decision. And in a broader sense a similar change took place in the family as a whole. All the neurotic denials, fears, and desires for revenge that had been absorbed in the young woman's illness were shown to be the responsibility of the man who had hitherto fobbed off his unsolved problem on the clinical case. It could be counted as an advance as well that a sham marriage, which was in fact a symptom in the family neurosis, was unmasked and dissolved.

This might be denied, of course, if one were to demand that family therapy necessarily be a therapy of integration, an education for unity at any price. That would be an authoritarian, ideological concept of family therapy which would not be in keeping with psychoanalytical principles. A psychoanalytical family therapist must not consider himself ideologically obligated to uphold the family. Naturally he does not fail to recognize the responsibility of patients who are trying to disrupt family unity. And he should not arbitrarily exclude the question of responsibility if it turns up in therapy. In the case being discussed, the marriage had been wrecked long before therapy began. A formal marriage still existed which in reality had not been a marriage at all for a long time. So the only question that remained was whether those involved would find the courage honestly to confess to themselves and to each other the situation they had created.

Thus concludes the report on this particular family therapy. In the description of the dynamics of the neurotic partner relationship and its change in the course of treatment, one point has had only incidental attention, yet it played a leading part in the medical reports on the young woman.

What kind of sickness did she really have? Which of the many expert medical diagnoses was right? hysteria? psychopathia? depression? hebephrenic schizophrenia?

Unquestionably, her localized physical symptoms were of a hysterical-conversion nature. In her personality structure as well, we find hysterical characteristics. But what about the severe instinctual disturbance that lasted for seven years? What about her withdrawal from her profession and from almost all social contacts outside the family? Why did she lie brooding on her sofa year in and year out like a person seriously ill? Here one might consider a depressive instinctual disturbance. And the progressive narrowing of her social contacts made it plausible to consider schizophrenic autism, though neither a true depression nor a psychosis of a schizophrenic nature had ever existed. It is worth noting how in this case the family conflict so overgrew and disguised a hysterical neurosis that one runs into trouble with the classical psychiatric diagnostic categories. And so it is understandable that confusion arose in the various neurological clinics when attempts were made to apply traditional psychiatric diagnostics to this patient. And it is significant that one diagnosis after another was made. In this process, mistaking a purely conflict-conditioned situation as a psychosis led to a most harmful step, the application of electro-shock therapy.

This, then, is one of those cases which show the inadequacy of the traditional one-sidedness of psychiatric thinking. Where psychic illnesses are the result and expression of group conflicts, they are misunderstood when an attempt is made simply to assign them to a place in the old psychiatric system of classification and to treat them accordingly. How grotesque must seem the wasteful dispute, going on for years, over the correctness of this or that classical individual diagnosis, while the group conflict supporting the illness progresses undiagnosed and untreated.

14

Domestic Duel—with Symptoms as Weapons

Referred to me by an internist colleague, a thirty-three-year-old driving instructor presents himself, smooth-shaven and youthful-looking:

"Two days before Christmas was when it began. A feeling as though I was about to faint, as if everything in me was going into convulsions. Pains in my heart, and a dreadful feeling of dizziness, too." "Later it hit me in the stomach, and I had diarrhea, too." "I belched a lot. The doctor said that came from swallowing air." This had been going on for months now, he said. He had been to two neurologists and an internist. Because of his heart, he had been given an electrocardiogram, but nothing significant had turned up. He really did not have a single day without pain: "As soon as I begin to brood, there is this spasm here." And he points to his breast and the upper part of his abdomen.

He mentions that his brother died of a cardiac infarct a year ago. "At the time I didn't shed a single tear, perhaps it has been eating into me?" He speaks of his mother too, who is just as nervous and fearful as he is. He announces of his own accord that he has no problem with his mother. "She does everything

and gives everything." Such extravagant praise of his mother is
sure to be followed immediately by severe criticism of someone
else, the therapist thinks to himself. And sure enough, the
patient next lets go at his wife, who causes him much vexation.
But she, too, is sick: "She is dreadfully tense. At night she
often cannot sleep, but I don't sleep well either." And then it
turns out that three days before the beginning of his sickness—
that is, five days before Christmas—his wife fainted dead away.
"She was dizzy and had a convulsive weeping attack that lasted
for hours. She has trouble with her back, too. The doctor told
her that because of her back it would be advisable for her not
to have children. As a matter of fact, I often have trouble
with my back, too."

The therapist thinks to himself: At almost the same time, both
have attacks of fainting, both suffer from cramps, both have
back trouble and sleep badly. How might these two illnesses fit
together?

The patient reveals more particulars about the difficulties in
his marriage. "When we have differences of opinion, she gets
cramps. And I have to talk for a long time before they let up."
"If I don't talk to her enough sometime, or if I happen to
raise my voice, she gets upset at once. Then she walks out. I
feel silly, because often I'm not to blame at all." "I give in
now a lot more than I used to. I simply can't stand it. I go to
pieces too quickly."

And then he describes how he is unable to endure any tension. "Perfectly unimportant misunderstandings throw me into
a state of confusion. It was that way before our marriage—if
we did not see each other for a single day, I was dreadfully
depressed. I get jealous about nothing at all and then I
immediately become dejected." "Sometimes I let my wife go
on vacation alone. Then my nervousness begins. What restless-
ness in my whole body! And there's no justification for it. My
wife hasn't anyone else and I don't think her capable of that.
But there's nothing I can do about it. I know that I get on her
nerves." "She always says that she is less ill when she's on
vacation than when she's at home with me."

But the wife too, he says, is very nervous. For example, she can't go out on the street after dark. She is afraid of night in general. Her inhibitions cause her many difficulties.

Once more, so the therapist notes, the patient is placing his wife in parallel to himself. Both are to a great extent fellow sufferers. They not only have similar pains and cramps but they are also similarly nervous. There is one difference. When they disagree, the wife apparently reacts stubbornly, stops talking, and goes away. He must run after her, even when he does not feel that he is at fault. She can go off alone, he can barely tolerate the separation. Now the question arises: What is the cause of the disagreements the husband speaks about repeatedly?

In the next interview he provides some information on the subject: "When she wants to buy something and I don't immediately say yes—then there's an explosion." "It's true I hardly ever bring her anything when I come home. But I think to myself, she gets plenty for herself." Then it emerges further that the husband worries often that the owner of the driving school will not retain him as a teacher. He is afraid that suddenly some day he will be without an income. His thoughts dwell on how long his money will last. He has managed to put away some savings. Obviously he has a neurotic anxiety about poverty. He describes himself as miserly, something his wife, he admits, often reproaches him for. She seems to provoke him on this painful point, but here he does not give in, although on all other subjects he does. His fear of financial distress is simply greater than his fear of his wife's susceptibility to illness and her silent obstinacy.

Here, evidently, is an area in which the wife runs after him and he withdraws. He tantalizes her by keeping out of reach what she wants. He is constantly afraid that she will not give him enough affection. And she is constantly afraid that he will not give her enough money.

The therapist now recalls that the illness of both patients struck shortly before Christmas. First the wife had a fainting fit. And then he had his neurotic cardiac attack, accompanied by feelings of faintness. Was all this perhaps also caused by worrying over money? Not until later sessions does it become clear that this intuition is correct. The husband was in a panic because the expenses for Christmas gifts had, in his opinion, reached a disturbing sum, and he had put his wife off about a specific request for her birthday, which was to follow shortly. Dreadfully agitated by this refusal, the wife had suffered the fainting fit and immediately afterward had fallen into a defiant silence. That had been the last straw for the husband. Even before this, he had been in a state of confusion because of the excessive expenses for Christmas. Short of money, with his wife's fainting fit on his conscience, and being punished in addition by her defiance—he was struck by a neurotic heart attack. A typical relief measure for a cardiac neurosis, as the literature shows.

The doctor concludes this interview with the patient by saying that he would like to invite the man's wife for a talk. It seems to him that joint marriage therapy is indicated, since the patient has really made it very clear that his illness and his wife's illness are presumably related to the continual conflicts they have with each other. But naturally, so therapist and patient agree, the wife must first be consulted.

The wife appears for the interview. She is a pretty, graceful blonde, but her regular, delicate features somehow seem tense and stiff. The word "rigid" used by the husband seems to the therapist very appropriate. She expresses herself more hesitantly and cautiously than her husband, obviously not just because she is irritated that he has already presented the problem from his point of view. It is easy to imagine that during an argument she would be the first to fall silent and withdraw.

Then she describes her ailments in detail, agreeing in general with the essentials of her husband's report. But plainly it is harder for her to see her symptoms in direct connection with her psychic problems. Her husband is far ahead of her in recognizing the connection. She sees her ailments rather as massive obstacles against which she feels helpless. They are like huge stones blocking her path. The therapist realizes that it will only gradually dawn on her that these may be the reversible effects of her inner psychic states. Working with her may turn out to be tougher than working with her husband—and this later proves to be true.

That her marriage is full of problems she sees well enough.

And she can express herself about them too, but only as though they were on a plane far removed from her sickness. She admits that she used to be merrier and more optimistic. "Something or other has changed completely. My nerves aren't good. Generally I feel out of sorts. My husband often criticizes me for this." Also, she is unhappy about living with her mother-in-law, who she feels does not give her proper recognition. "But for the sake of peace in the household, I cannot mention that to my husband. He always says his mother means well in everything." "My mother-in-law criticizes me as though I were a little child. It begins with the way I dress and ends with the way I hold my spoon. Everything is supervised and criticized." "I can't stand these rebukes any longer." At night she has attacks of dread and usually has to leave the lights on. Then she talks about how she is always self-conscious. That is so in her sexual relations too. She cannot even talk easily with her husband. This is something that has caught her mother-in-law's attention.

She describes herself—so it seems to the therapist—as if she were a child who is supposed to try constantly to do things right and produce something worthwhile. But she feels that she does everything wrong, produces nothing of value, and has no recognized position in the household or anywhere else. She is under constant pressure, but she is pretty much resigned to it.

Earlier, her husband had understood her even less than now. "But recently things are going a little better. Now that he himself has caught the sickness, it is easier for him to sympathize with me. Now he can see for himself what something like this can be like."

Concerning the quarrels about money, purchases, and gifts, she volunteers nothing on this occasion. But the subject will come up all the more obsessively during the treatment. For her it is obviously still too explosive, and therefore it remains repressed for now.

In the course of the interview, the woman becomes somewhat more communicative and sympathetic. Also, her facial expression loses some of its rigidity, though any suggestion of hope is still barely perceptible. Nevertheless, she agrees to join her husband in joint marriage therapy.

In the first joint session, it emerges more clearly than before that both husband and wife are trying to use their symptoms, each to his or her own advantage. The symptoms are a means of expression for various things: for pleas, threats, and punishment. The husband at the moment complains chiefly about his heart; the woman, about her back and a lack of sleep. They seldom criticize each other in words, especially outside the sessions. But every time one of them feels neglected or offended, his ailments grow worse. This happens because each is reacting neurotically to the symptoms of the other. An unspoken dialogue something like this is acted out:

"You are mean to me! Now just look, I get sicker right away!" To this, the other's reaction is: "If you are trying to punish me through your sickness, then you've miscalculated. Just look at me: today I am in much worse pain than you!" In the complaints, however, there is also a plea: "You must take better care of me! Look how much I suffer!" Then the other: "But how can I do that, my suffering is much greater, and it doesn't move you at all!" And so this is a contest in more senses than one. Who is the greater martyr and entitled to denounce the other as a cruel oppressor? Who has the greater right to be the other's patient, who must play the part of nurse?

In the course of this subterranean battle, it happens, interestingly enough, that each of them approximates his complaints to those of the other. The husband talks less about his heart; instead, they both emphasize their aching backs and troubled sleep. Also, both see a parallel in the fact that neither can watch horror films. In general, they avoid crime and adventure movies entirely, but now they have experimented with a suspense film on television. At one place in the film a hand came out of an open coffin. They had to turn off the set. In the same session the husband reports other fears. He has a constriction in his nose and has trouble breathing properly. This causes him anxiety. Does he perhaps suffer feelings of suffocation at night? Also, he is apprehensive about a little test he will soon have to take. In addition he is alarmed whenever, during a driving lesson, a pupil speaks of being ill; he would really like to stop the car and run away. Whereupon the wife takes over the conversation and talks about her night fears. She is frightened, too, before each of the therapy sessions. In the waiting room she has to get hold of herself to keep from trembling.

And so, in respect to being afraid, neither will yield to the other. In the psychic as in the physical realm, neither will admit to less suffering. The therapist voices this impression. He points out to both that obviously it is a matter of importance for one not to be healthier and stronger than the other, and vice versa. Just as though that were something to be ashamed of, or something that would require one to do more for the other. The therapist repeats this interpretation a number of times, at whatever points this kind of rivalry emerges most clearly during the treatment.

After a number of sessions, a remarkable change takes place: the man announces with great satisfaction that things are very much better with him now. His pains have almost disappeared. "There is no comparison to what it was like before." The behavior of the woman, when the man for the first time reveals his improvement, is especially surly and withdrawn. She hardly speaks at all and creates an oppressive atmosphere which visibly intimidates her husband. Toward the therapist, too, she is markedly hostile. One can feel her reproach: "You've helped my husband, but you've done nothing for me."

In any case, it is perfectly clear that she feels her husband's improvement is a challenge. But the husband, whom she irritates once more through her strong opposition, does not let himself worry to the extent of collapsing into his earlier, customary doleful state. His symptoms remain improved, even though his wife gives more vivid expression to her own ills. His increased resistance finally leads to her realization that she must change her method. Since the silent demonstration of suffering has awakened no echo, her anger bursts out in words. She becomes vastly more talkative, and lively word battles result. In this way, an entirely new scene is staged: they no longer fight chiefly with symptoms; they battle verbally.

The principal theme of the sessions ceases to be the physical suffering on either side and becomes the conflict resulting from the manifold grievances that each nourishes against the other. In the course of these arguments, the wife even complains to the husband: "It was easier to live with you when you were sicker." Whereupon he says: "Should I perhaps have more pain again, just so you can understand me better?"

As is the case often in marriage therapy, this pair is stimulated by the treatment to continue discussing at home the problems raised during the sessions. Especially on the night before a session, there are heated arguments in which the actual session to come is in a sense composed in advance. An hour begins as follows:

He: Things go up and down with me. On the whole, though, it is much better.

She: Yesterday I couldn't help weeping a great deal again.

(*Pause.*)

Therapist: Would you mind saying what you wept about?

She: Let him say it!

He: We had it out again yesterday. That's getting to be almost a habit the night before we come here. Then everything from the past comes to the surface. My wife simply thinks that I'm a horrible person. Yesterday she said again that it could never get better unless I change entirely. Sometimes I say no when she wants something. She insists that I must always agree to everything.

She: It always has to be the way he says. He never lets me have my way. Yesterday I held up my brother-in-law as an example, how generous he is with his wife although they are no better off than we are. Thirty marks pocket money—that's all I get. Yet I really have no extravagant tastes. If only he weren't so suspicious of me! (*She cries.*)

He: You simply never notice the attention I pay you.

She: No!

Therapist: Neither of you believes the other wants to be kind and neither will meet the other halfway.

He: Yes, I do want to sometimes, but then she simply turns the other way.

She: Yes, because he's so coarse.

(*Short pause.*)

He: Actually, it's mostly about buying or not buying. She has a friend who always has to have the newest thing in clothes. All the neighbors admire them. So my wife thinks she has to be like her . . .

I used to go shopping with her sometimes. If I pointed out something that I thought would be becoming, she would say: "You picked that out for me just because it's so cheap." (*She continues to cry and is silent.*)

At this time the sessions produce, as indicated, a lot of quarreling. In this the wife now seems more aggressive, the husband more defensive. He does more of the talking, but much of what he says sounds apologetic. The arguments on both sides seldom vary. Nevertheless, the therapist notes as an advance that a continuing dialogue has sprung up and that the original battle with physical symptoms as weapons no longer dominates the scene as it did formerly. The therapist considers it his duty to keep this dialogue going. He feels that the couple, despite their sadomasochistic traits, despite the mutual torment they have caused, do not want to drive each other completely mad. They need each other too much for that. But like stubborn children, neither one ventures to express his need of the other's love in affectionate fashion instead of in the form of extortion.

Yet it can be observed that both are growing weary of their exchange of blows and are beginning to wonder: Why are we behaving like this?

Sometimes both husband and wife talk about their childhoods. As children, both felt at a disadvantage when compared to their siblings. He complains of the fact that his more robust brothers got on much better with the father. They knew how to ingratiate themselves with the mother as well. His mother had been sickly, domineering, and troublesome. The brothers refused to take her into their homes even temporarily but just the same they meant at least as much to her as he did. All they had to do was to come fawning around her once in a while and they got anything they wanted from her.

And the patient does not get everything from her? He must do a lot to purchase his mother's favor? One can see that he is hesitantly beginning to question the idealized description he gave in the first interview: she does everything and gives everything. With this idealization he had obviously for a long time repressed his indignation toward his mother, who actually did too little and gave too little. And in order to keep this indignation repressed, he could not permit his wife's slightest criticism of his mother to go unchallenged. His fear of endangering the painfully won understanding with his mother drove him so far as to assist her in her jealous domination over his wife. In one session he brings himself to admit: "I don't dare bring my wife flowers because if I did my mother would be jealous. I can never kiss my wife, either, as long as my mother is around." His miserliness toward his wife, which offends her so gravely, reveals itself, in the course of the treatment, to be a sacrifice to his mother. Every deprecation of his wife desired by his mother is acceptable to him simply for the frantic preservation of the illusion of a completely satisfying relationship with his essentially terribly feared and hated mother.

Naturally, it is a great relief to the young wife when she sees the husband admit for the first time some of his repressed resentment toward his mother. *She:* I've often told you the family make you a black sheep and you shouldn't put up with it. But you would never admit it.

By chance, during this phase of the treatment, the mother goes on a trip. This seems to make it easier for the husband to express his critical feelings for her in more detail. The wife adds: "Now that my mother-in-law is away, things are going much better with us." The husband comments: "Yes, I too find it agreeable to have a little more room to move about."

Whereas in the beginning he had always interrupted her if she said anything critical about his mother, now he is able just to let it pass. The feeling that the wife is automatically attacking him when criticizing his mother has lessened. Instead, he begins to see that the wife is not rejecting him but is trying to woo him when she attempts to rival the mother.

The wife feels that she will benefit from this slowly developing process of self-understanding on the part of the husband. To the extent that he begins to question his mother and the other members of the family, he grows closer to her. She rewards him

by offering him more signs of conciliatory reasonableness. And
so even the most explosive subject of their chronic marriage conflict, which hitherto, like a red flag, had been the signal for instant attack, finally becomes accessible to a rational approach:
his, in her eyes, inhuman avarice and her, in his eyes, limitless
extravagance. One day she is able to admit that she has exaggerated her greediness in order to provoke him. "If only he
didn't always get so angry, I would not have mentioned a lot of
things I wanted." In return for this, he admits that he has
neglected her because of his mother and says that in the future
he intends to change.

Naturally, these self-critical confessions are voiced only cautiously and by degrees. And there remain all sorts of tension
points that delay a complete understanding between the two.
But movement has begun in this congealed relationship and it
progresses steadily. "We have never in our whole marriage
talked so much about our problems as now," the wife declares.
He gives her more money and observes that she does not in
fact spend any more than before. "I always knew, of course, that
she was really economical. But I just couldn't give her any
more. I was suspicious, though I had no reason to be." She, on
her side, encourages him about the test that he has to take. She
also furnishes another proof that she wants greater closeness:
shortly before the end of the treatment, she comes out with the
fact that, after all, she would like to have a child and she does
not think her back trouble is necessarily an obstacle.

Sure enough, examination by specialists confirms that from a
physical point of view there need be no hesitation about a preg-
nancy. The husband is very happy about the wife's desire for a
child and he understands precisely the affectionate background
of this offer, the melting of her defiant coldness. Each is at least
trying to give up his neurotic weapons, because the growing
mutual understanding is reducing their original, morbidly exaggerated distrust.

After about seven months, the couple decide that they can end
the treatment, at least for a while. His ailments have completely disappeared; hers have substantially improved. Unquestionably, the two people, now that they have learned to

discuss their difficulties outside the treatment, have a better chance of solving their problems in the future without being forced to take refuge blindly in an irrational duel of symptoms.

The therapist would like to have continued this rewarding treatment for a while longer, in order to make use of the dynamics of the process set in motion to achieve a more complete stabilization of the situation. In any case, each of the two people, because of his own character and because of the configuration of their common conflict, offered the possibility of going quite a bit further in analytical work. It was one of those instances in which the therapist almost regrets that the symptoms improve rapidly, depriving the patient of his motive for enduring the distress of the additional treatment that would be advisable to assure stabilization. On the other hand, because one is a psychotherapist, one should keep one's perfectionism in check, for it is up to those being treated to decide how far they wish to proceed with the analytical process and where they want to call a halt.

15

"Simple Counseling"
A BLACK SHEEP IS TAKEN INTO THE FOLD

Even in a broad concept of family therapy, one has to describe as "counseling" the procedure used in the next case. This family was seen at long intervals only and their conflicts were not analytically worked through with the help of interpretations and explanations. The doctor limited himself to listening, to making supportive comments and, much more rarely, interpretations. Moreover, at a number of points he actively intervened with practical help. The infrequency of the contact, the absence of any systematic arrangement for treatment, and the doctor's reliance more on support than on the analytical working through of the problems indicate a form of activity on the part of the doctor that is most accurately termed "counseling." The psychotherapist was not the only one to provide help but was associated with a number of social workers, each of whom contributed substantially to the success of this laborious but gratifying family treatment.

The wife of a steamfitter's assistant brings her seven-year-old son, Michael, to the consulting room. The youngster says almost nothing, and that little very unclearly. He is strikingly awkward in his movements. Intellectually, he is several years behind his contemporaries. He is able to recognize and call by name only a few toys. In the school for children with speech defects where he has been placed because of his problems of articulation, he cannot keep up with the instruction. But, beyond all this, Michael's mother is disturbed by his inconsiderate and often distressing behavior: he likes to quarrel with other children and spits in their faces. At home, when he is angered at being corrected, he sometimes smashes a cup or a plate. He makes faces at his mother. Among his classmates he creates so much disturbance and shows so much aggression that the teacher and the principal have asked his mother and the Bureau of Education to take Michael out of the school. In the family, too, it no longer seems possible to put up with him. At least his stepfather is no longer willing to let him stay in the house.

His mother, a simple, emotional woman, cannot restrain her tears after she has reported this apparently hopeless situation. A further complication in family relationships is that Michael is an illegitimate child, born before his mother's marriage to her present husband. His real father was—according to the mother —a "no-account." She did not realize this until she was pregnant; the relationship had quickly broken up. The father sends money for support very irregularly. They have had to apply repeatedly to the Child Welfare Department for help.

Her present husband, Michael's stepfather, is, to be sure, severe, but he means well. However, he can no longer endure Michael's behavior and the complaints about the boy that come in from all sides. He thinks it would be best for Michael to be sent to a home for defective children, and the school has confirmed this opinion. The mother is most unhappy about the predicament. She believes that at bottom Michael is a very lovable youngster who on account of his intellectual shortcomings feels inferior and rejected and simply for this reason reacts so aggressively. She will let him leave their house only as a last resort: "My husband has already told me twice, 'Either he goes or I go myself. You have to make up your mind.' "

She dares not intercede for Michael with her husband any more. Recently, he indicated to her that he had made enough sacrifices for this youngster who was not even his own flesh and blood. This had wounded her so much that she now feels utterly helpless. Indeed, she thinks that she is responsible, that her husband is having to pay for her mistake. She loves her husband and does not want to endanger their marriage. But she does not see how the problem of calming him is to be solved without sending the boy away.

Michael is in fact a sick child. His disturbance is not simply the expression of a neurotic family conflict but the result of a congenital—or at least very early acquired—brain injury. The damage to the brain has already been established by several neurologists. In the course of a confirming neurological examination, the therapist records the same deficiencies: the so-called physiological tendon reflexes are exaggerated and not bilaterally symmetrical. Also, the results of an electro-encephalogram are disturbing.

The youngster has an asymmetrical face, which makes his features look crooked and somewhat distorted. His faint, indistinct speech complicates communication, which his limited vocabulary and general confusion of mind make very difficult anyway. Usually he looks as though he were leering in a seemingly unfriendly way. But since his facial expressions are not under complete control and especially cannot be symmetrically moved, this "hostile" appearance is misleading. Only after a number of sessions with Michael does it become clear that his leer is really an embarrassed smile. He still behaves with a small child's timidity, but he is obviously trying to get used to the doctor and to please him.

In a test with blocks, because of his awkward movements he has trouble setting up anything without knocking it down again at once. For a while he pushes a little racing car around on the floor, growling. He calls the car a "roller." In an examination of his muscular control (moto-metric test), it turns out that in the development of coordinated movement he is substantially behind the average for his age. This difference corresponds approximately to the degree of his intellectual retardation. But by Michael's second visit the therapist is aware that the boy is becoming increasingly trustful and is losing much of the anxiety that was clearly evident at first. He is obviously grateful that he is not scolded and that he is allowed to play unimpeded. He begins to grow familiar with the new environment.

The mother, for her part, is very happy that the youngster is received here in so friendly a manner. She, too, appears to have changed by the second visit. She gives the impression of being somewhat more confident and hopeful. It clearly encourages her that she does not immediately have to listen to bad reports about the boy, that for once her problem and his are treated with good will and patience, and that she has found a readiness to be helpful.

Meanwhile, it becomes evident that this woman, who like her husband comes from a simple working-class background, is emotionally a discriminating and sensitive person; her courage in facing her fate with her sick son impresses the therapist. He feels that in this mother he has a reliable ally who, in spite of all the difficulties that must be anticipated with Michael, will not easily capitulate if only she finds some support from outside.

After the tedious examination of the boy over the course of a number of visits has been concluded, the stepfather is invited in for a consultation. It is easy to see that he is inclined to severity. He recounts a series of especially upsetting misdeeds that Michael had been guilty of in kindergarten and especially more recently in school. But at home, too, all is not well; Michael is beginning to torment his little half sister (the child of the present marriage) when he thinks he is unobserved. He sticks his tongue out at his mother and partly intentionally and partly out of clumsiness breaks a great many things.

The family is living, it appears, in a crowded, two-room apartment in an old, dilapidated house. The pay of a steamfitter's assistant is small. Michael ruins his clothes in no time, breaks household objects, and thus adds unwarranted expense to the many other irritations. The stepfather, who in other respects seems not unreasonable, betrays a certain amount of bitterness in describing his difficulties with Michael. And it is easy to see that he feels put upon and would really like to say: "Please understand that I can no longer carry this undeserved responsibility. You may appeal to my sense of duty. But I really can't manage it any more."

The doctor does not appeal to his sense of duty but shows that he recognizes the difficulties and is very much impressed with what the stepfather has already put up with. And Michael's mother, the therapist adds, has also expressed herself as being very moved by how patiently and considerately the stepfather has behaved toward the youngster, although he has had to endure so many disappointments in him.

The man is touched by this praise and grows thoughtful. If at first he was bent on self-defense, now he is prepared to consider, together with his wife and the therapist, what chances there may be of improving this miserable situation.

The first thing to be settled is the question of school. The parents have been informed that as a result of psychological tests the youngster has been judged unfit for the school for children with speech defects and belongs, rather, in a home for the retarded, because his speech difficulties are only part of his general intellectual retardation. Since his dismissal from the school for speech defects is unavoidable, his acceptance in a special home must be arranged at once. The therapist tells Michael's parents that he will use his influence to obtain Michael's admittance.

Most pressing, of course, is the decision whether to follow the recommendation to commit the boy to a home or whether the mother and stepfather might still see the possibility of giving Michael one more chance with them. In the latter case, the therapist suggests treating the boy as an outpatient in the future, so that he might exercise some influence on his disturbed behavior. Of course, one must not expect too much from these efforts, since the organic nerve damage cannot be repaired.

In the ensuing conversation between husband and wife, Michael's mother indicates that she hopes they will accept the therapist's offer. Her husband expresses his doubts. He reminds her that the boy has already had a bad effect on his little sister. The mother interjects that perhaps Michael is only jealous of his sister, and moreover she believes the boy is incapable of doing his sister any harm. He probably would not become physically violent, the father admits. But can she, the mother, put up with his insolent behavior—the way he sticks his tongue out

at her and gives way to destructive rages? The stepfather at any
rate has had enough of it, as well as of the constant irritation of
the irregular support payments from the boy's real father. *He*
had got away scot-free, didn't have a thing to worry about,
whereas they between them had to bear the brunt of it all.

The mother does not reply. Her husband turns to the
therapist: Might not Michael improve in a special home? The
therapist expresses his opinion that the boy, because of his
disability, would certainly not have an easy time of it making a
place for himself in a special home, where he could not possibly
receive as intensive and kind attention as with his family. But if
the stepfather cannot endure Michael at home, then there is no
other course.

The stepfather asks for time to think it over. On the next visit
the mother comes alone and announces, beaming, that her
husband has agreed again to reject for the time being the recommendation that Michael be committed to a special home. The
therapist thereupon makes an application to the Child Welfare
Department for support money for the boy. This application
has been carefully prepared for in advance with the directress of
the department, which has exercised guardianship over Michael
and is well acquainted with the case. The department is ready to
give sympathetic consideration to the application for support.
The argument that Michael, for the reasons mentioned, costs
his stepfather more money than a healthy child is accepted. The
directress understands, moreover, that the money has psychological importance as well. The stepfather struggling with this
burden would regard such concrete help as evidence that his
sacrifices for the disturbed boy are appreciated, and he will be
grateful and relieved.

The support allowance is granted. Although not specifically
invited, the stepfather accompanies his wife and Michael to the
next session. His attitude in comparison with that of the first
visit is hardly recognizable. No blustering, no embittered accusations. He seems on the whole ashamed of his accusatory manner
during the first visit and today is trying to make up for it. He is
at pains to communicate all sorts of kind things about Michael;
much to his wife's delight, he zealously praises the boy. With

visible embarrassment, he thanks the doctor for having secured the support allowance. In halting words he manages to say that this is the first time anyone has really helped him. "Up to now, all I've heard is a lot of talk."

At any rate, it is clear that he has finally been persuaded to cooperate. While asserting that with Michael things are "already going a little better," he obviously wants to show: I have made some improvement in myself, too. Now I am trying to see the good side of the youngster and I am making a special effort to put up with his crazy behavior more patiently.

This turnaround on the part of the stepfather ushered in treatment for this family that lasted over seven years. Despite many serious relapses on Michael's part, which will be mentioned later, the mother and stepfather—with the assistance of the therapist—worked out the boy's problems at home—that is, without resorting to a home for the retarded. In spite of the original impression he made, the stepfather overcame the diverse, unavoidable setbacks with admirable patience, always supporting the boy and helping him to an astonishingly positive development in view of the existing brain damage.

A few more details about the family history are necessary in order to appreciate fully the significance of the turning point that marked the real beginning of the family treatment.

They were faced with having to expel a brain-damaged child because of his social unacceptability. The stepfather correctly realized that endless sacrifice would be exacted from him because of this youngster in the middle of a crowded family life. Failures at school, complaints from the neighbors, frequent disturbances of the household peace, a handicap for the healthy little sister, additional expense, and many more annoyances were inevitable. And he did not see why he, as stepfather, should take all this upon himself for a stranger's child. School and youth authorities were ready to facilitate the desired removal of the boy. At the same time it was highly likely that after leaving the family figures that he knows so well, this helpless, infantile youngster would forfeit even more of his stability, that in a home for the retarded his character development would be considerably more threatened. But the stepfather, on whom the decision depended, changed as we have seen. And seemingly, what caused this change was in particular a single social act: the granting of the support allowance.

But was it money alone? Years of association with the family proved that this allowance meant far more to the stepfather than concrete financial assistance, important though that was. He is a man who wants to be good. He needs to feel of some account and is willing to make an effort toward that end. It was for this reason that he married a woman who, for all her simplicity of character, put greater demands on his intelligence. And so it is especially in her eyes and to her that he wants to be good. But he is also an impulsive fellow with strong instincts. He has aggressions. And this weak-minded, ugly, often sadistic youngster provokes in him exactly those instinctual impulses that he secretly judges disgraceful: he would like to punish the boy; inwardly, he would like to take revenge on the boy's father— yes, also on his wife, out of irrational jealousy.

In psychoanalytic translation, one might say he wants to throw the youngster out because the boy provokes in him the shameful, wicked aspects of his Self. It is as though Michael's presence prevents him from living out of the good side of his Self. In this dilemma, it happens that someone appeals to his secret ideal, his "good self," and strengthens this side of him. Here is someone who gives him recognition for his past sacrifices and efforts on the boy's behalf. The therapist shows that he does not take seriously the side that the stepfather superficially exhibits: the disappointed, angry, egotistic husband. Instead, the therapist addresses himself to the opposite, hidden side, the sensitive human being with high standards of value.

This striking result is possible, of course, only because this opposite, hidden side with which the therapist makes contact actually exists. In retrospect, one understands how this man had thirsted for a long time for some message from outside that was not a humiliating reprimand, warning, or report of disgrace and failure on the part of the boy—reproaches which the stepfather in his sensitiveness always felt were directed against himself. All that was needed was one man whom he respected—together with the wife—to restore his belief in the worthwhile side of his Self, which he had no longer had the strength to rely upon, someone to help him rediscover the pride of being able to do something especially good.

The psychotherapeutic and social assistance was effective because the recipient had especially favorable character traits. In addition, the assistance came at a moment of depressive instability when he was particularly open to this kind of encouragement. Without such psychological preconditions, similar supportive therapy offered daily in the consultation rooms of psychiatrists and the offices of educational advisers vanish like so much air, without any permanent effect.

But after that, other people besides the therapist had to intervene frequently in similar ways in order to help the stepfather persist.

As a stroke of good fortune, Michael falls into the hands of a completely understanding special-school teacher. At first, all his disciplinary difficulties are repeated with disturbing frequency: he suddenly turns the lights off and on during class, throws open the windows, climbs on the desks. He is often involved in fistfights in which he often has to take a beating. At times, too, he hits himself in the face and shouts at himself: "You're a dope, you're just a dope!"

All this causes considerable disturbance in the class—but the teacher sticks by him with patience that borders on the miraculous. She often discusses him with the doctor. They agree that they should keep on trying to get Michael through the period of difficulty caused by his entering a new school. In fact, the boy gradually improves. And the mother, who comes for regular sessions, is happy when she can report not just new incidents but improvements. She comments thankfully on the understanding support of her husband. And she expresses the opinion that the treatment has rescued not only the boy but her marriage as well.

Eventually, the class no longer regards Michael simply as a troublemaker and stops picking on him. Instead, they accept him as a kind of class clown. His ugly faces and little tricks are seldom taken as provocative now. The children are amused by them. And he in turn learns that playing the clown is not so bad. Basically good-humored, he is even grateful for the applause and laughter of the group. If people just won't torment him, then he has no call to be mischievous. He is happy to be egged on to do something funny for the entertainment of the others. This particular docility, however, later proves to be not without danger.

For the moment, however, aside from isolated untoward incidents, his development is quite satisfactory. His speech slowly improves. He finds it easier to make himself understood. Toward his little sister he develops an affectionate attitude, since mother and stepfather are especially careful to give him the least possible cause for jealousy. In the special school he makes a creditable record in various subjects, particularly arithmetic. His mother is very proud of this. But his insufficient self-control causes him again and again to become aggressive. Once he is on the point of striking his teacher with his fist. The rector wants Michael expelled from school. Yet the remarkably patient and determined teacher remains loyal to the boy. Actually, after his occasional outbursts he usually gets hold of himself quickly again. The cooperation between mother, stepfather, teacher, directress, and doctor continues through many difficult situations—caused by various misdeeds of Michael's—in which, from one quarter or another, the question of confining him in an institutional home is raised.

But, through the period of prepuberty, the difficulties continue to decrease. By arrangement, the intervals between therapeutic sessions are steadily lengthened. On one occasion—Michael is twelve at the time—the mother announces that today she wants to show only how irreproachably things are going with her son. She exhibits a quite acceptable report card. With special satisfaction, she points to the commendation for good conduct. "It's true he's still a little defiant. He doesn't obey me nearly so well as he does my husband." But in general both she and her husband are very pleased.

During his meetings with the doctor, Michael behaves with increasing confidence and greater understanding. It is now possible to discuss with him simple aspects of the case—for example, his anger at his fellow students, his conflict with the teachers, and controversies at home.

But then the boy comes into puberty and, as was to be expected, his difficulties increase once more. Urged on by two schoolmates, he takes part in the theft of a bicycle. The two others show him how it is done. Later, on orders from these two, he steals mirrors and tool kits from other bicycles in order to equip the stolen one. Naïvely, he brags in class about his daring acts—and is promptly reported. There follow painful hearings at the police station. The stepfather, summoned by the police and by the school, has to listen to stern, unpleasant reprimands because of these misdeeds. This is a delicate test of strength for him, which he passes admirably. Instead of joining in the general condemnation of the boy, he busies himself more intensively from then on and skillfully helps Michael to break with his criminal companions. The directress of Child Welfare intercedes with the police on Michael's behalf and succeeds in keeping them from harrying him. And the therapist does his part in helping the boy get over these difficult incidents. It turns out that Michael had hardly realized the harm he was doing to other people through thefts of this sort. What meant more to him was the recognition he received from his brighter companions for his willingness to help. Even the stolen bicycle awakened in him simply a small child's joy. It was obvious that at this time he was incapable of discriminating, of moral judgments.

Yet he succeeds in freeing himself completely from both of the real culprits. No further thefts or other misdeeds take place. To be sure, his mother and stepfather notice with anxiety that other ruffians in the neighborhood attempt to win Michael's friendship. His weak intelligence and his suggestibility make him especially attractive to rascals looking for helpers in their shady business. And in the neighborhood around the family apartment there is no lack of bad characters. Up to the end of the treatment, however, no further incidents occur. The next-to-last report card of the school year shows, on the whole, adequate achievement. Michael's conduct continues to be criticized but in much milder form than in earlier reports. As for his responsible behavior at home, the mother's laudatory comments on Michael's performance of household duties speaks for itself. On the whole, it seems astonishing that Michael has been able to get so far in school and it looks as if he will finish satisfactorily.

In retrospect, this case history is not an example of the healing of a sickness. But it shows how a family on the verge of a breakup can deal with a problem that made extremely heavy demands. The family performed a considerable achievement: enabling a boy with irreparable brain damage, feebleminded, and in grave danger of degeneration, to maintain the greatest control possible, allowing him to attain as much social solidarity as was possible in view of his handicap. And, according to all observations, the family has done this without becoming neurotically warped in its inner structure, as for example was the case with the businessman's family (see chapter 7) and as is seen daily in similar situations.

It is a most extraordinary outcome: this boy with so little control because of organic deficiencies, impulsive, intellectually retarded, could be kept not only in the family but also in school and as part of school society. Had he suffered, as he almost did, a series of rejections—by his family, by the school, possibly by several homes for the retarded—it is highly probable that he would long since have been doomed to isolation as a hopeless case and would be vegetating his life away in an asylum, a wreck of humanity.

It would be inadequate, however, to measure the accomplishment of this family simply by the success of Michael's development. The husband and wife during these difficult years have themselves achieved an admirable advance. Through their stouthearted persistence in their task, each has won self-respect for himself; and their union, so seriously threatened originally, has become firm. About the stepfather there is only indirect evidence, since during the later years only Michael's mother continued to see the therapist. All the evidence, however, points to the fact that out of this wobbly marriage, constantly threatened by the impulse-ridden husband, has emerged a marriage of remarkable durability.

Incidentally, it should be noted that this and similar cases refute the prejudice that families with little education are generally more inclined to act out their problems in primitive fashion than are families with a better education. The achievement of this uneducated workman and his simple wife in guiding the sick boy Michael is far above that of many other families in favored social circumstances when faced with a similar situation. As a family therapist, one learns through experience that particularly in workers' families one often finds a readiness for especially open and self-critical cooperation. This is so not only with the counseling type of procedure, such as was used in Michael's case, but generally too when the more differentiated techniques of psychoanalytical family therapy in the narrower sense are called for (see chapter 10).

16

Where Family Therapy May Fail

As a comparatively new psychotherapeutic treatment, family therapy has not yet been fully explored and often, for extrinsic reasons, it is very difficult to apply. In the West German Republic there are probably no more than a handful of psychotherapists who make a systematic practice of family therapy. Thus a warning to pay strict regard to its limitations would hardly seem necessary. More often than not, a case that clearly calls for family therapy is shunted to less promising treatment in individual psychotherapy. As yet, family therapy is anything but the fashion, and it is an open question whether it ever will be. The amount of time, the expense, and, for the therapist, the much more complicated determination of the problem as compared with individual therapy unquestionably interfere substantially with its development. At the moment, therefore, it would seem justified to present the objectively worthwhile family-therapy method as optimistically as possible to make its potentialities emphatically clear to patients, therapists, and those who bear the expense.

Nevertheless, with what is after all a radical medical treatment, too much is at stake for one to dare promote it for uncritical experimentation. For this reason, it is important to note certain specific difficulties that are sometimes overlooked in determining whether family therapy is needed.

Special attention should be paid to a family type that seems to offer itself for family therapy more conspicuously than any other, yet if one ventures to apply this therapy one usually and very quickly encounters obstacles that are extremely difficult to overcome.

This is the family that has polarized itself into two parts that exhibit strong tension toward each other. Both sides come to see the therapist in the hope—so at least they say—that he will help them settle a debatable problem that they have in common. They intentionally betray nothing of the fact that they unconsciously promise themselves a settlement of their problem by forcing the therapist to fail. Sometimes, for example, it is a child showing evidences of neglect, or with psychosomatic symptoms, concerning whose upbringing a battle is raging that has brought the parents to seek advice. Or a married couple quarreling because each believes he or she is badly treated by the other. Often both have neurotic symptoms for which each blames the other. At first glance, one might think that here family treatment is an obvious possibility, for one of the principal prerequisites mentioned earlier is clearly fulfilled: the family has a common problem and the members of the family expressly declare that they are seeking help.

But this is not enough. It is also essential to determine whether those involved seem ready and capable of reliably sustaining intensive work on the problem together with the therapist.

Well, what about this particular prerequisite in the case of the polarized, embattled family? Will the members of the family who are at odds promise to cooperate? At this point the reader, recalling some of the case histories cited, may believe that, even in the case of serious family differences, an adroit therapist should be able to succeed in interesting these people in open participation in the treatment. But this would be a dangerous assumption. As in every prospective family therapy case, it is desirable, but especially with the typical embattled family, to make a careful investigation of how the family has hitherto tried to deal with its common problems.

Has the family already worked on serious problems for a long period and solved them? Was it capable of sustaining internal tension without serious effects? Has the family shown the strength to withstand such blows of fate as severe illness, professional reverses, and financial losses? Most important of all: is there some kind of a reliable basic contact beneath the superficial bickerings and grumblings?

There is also an important series of professional questions: How has the family behaved in the past toward advisers from outside, arbiters and doctors? How, for example, do they talk about their earlier treatment by therapists, educational advisers, or social workers? Are they quick to look for outside help, or do they decide on it only in cases of necessity? Are they inclined to submit passively to outside authorities, or are they simply seeking suggestions and advice about matters for which they will make themselves responsible in the end? Or does this family habitually do both, one after the other? That is, first submit to an outside helper and build him up as an absolute authority, only to become quickly disillusioned, turn away, and reject him?

It is this last reaction discovered through a careful examination of the previous history that can fairly often reveal a typical "embattled family." They remark, let us say, on the great confidence with which they placed themselves in the care of this or that specialist. But this confidence has always been bitterly disappointed. They sacrificed time, money, etc., and afterward everything was much worse than before. That specialist failed completely—on this point there is striking unanimity in the family despite all other differences, as one discovers from their emphatic and repeated assertions.

The family that reports experiences like this is inclined to believe that the new therapist can be easily influenced by such accounts to place himself at their disposal as a helper. The pathetic failure of his predecessors will—so they think—spur his ambition. After all, it cannot but flatter him to have this family, as though with flying colors, rush to join him, having completely broken with his earlier rivals.

An experienced psychoanalyst, however, will regard this form of ingratiation with special skepticism. If a family has no good word to say for the previous helpers they have sought out, then there is every likelihood that after a fleeting phase of respectful submission they will deprecate him in the same way and dismiss him. And this will be the result not of consciously infamous design but of an unconscious defensiveness. There are families that only through the periodic staging of this sort of play can regain for a time their equilibrium. Over a period of decades they may run through a gamut of outside advisers, each of whom they greet with great hopes and unexpressed wishes, and thereafter collectively denounce and leave in the lurch. This is their only means of dealing with their unmastered active aggressions: at those times when they are threatened with self-destruction by their reciprocal, hostile impulses, they quickly get hold of an outside authority, a doctor or perhaps at times a friend whom they elect as a kind of arbiter. Each part of the family firmly expects that through flattery it can draw this helper over to its side as a companion-in-arms. If then it finds the arbiter trying to perform his role of helper with unbiased neutrality, it feels itself rejected, just as the opposing part of the family does. And in both aggression-laden sections of the family it is now a temptation to deny their enmity toward each other and shift it to the person they had so eagerly wooed.

There are families of this type with which a therapist, however adroit he may be, has a hard time steering his therapeutic efforts so as to avoid exactly this outcome. If a family is thoroughly practiced in this game—sometimes over years—the therapist may turn and twist as he will; he is nevertheless forced with virtuoso skill into the role of courted helper who very quickly is transformed into a miserable whipping boy.

Of course, if a therapist is courageous enough and exceptionally invulnerable, he can make use of these predictable possibilities of the transference in order to gain experience and sometimes, despite everything, to achieve a very modest, partial therapeutic success. This assumes, to be sure, that he will strictly avoid allowing himself to be built up as the potential, unique savior of the betrayed and disillusioned, so as not to fall into the trap of the family's method. Once the therapist snaps up the proffered transference with obvious feelings of sympathy, he has already lost the game.

Another type of family that generally presents the family

therapist with special though not insuperable difficulties is the paranoid family, as shown in detail in chapter 7. This family is impressive mostly because of its solidarity, forcibly maintained though that may be. It makes use of an overrated idea or ideology to cut itself. off from its surroundings. This polarization against the outer world always has a definitely aggressive character, even if the aggression is concealed by a process of resentment formation. It may appear that there is no collective conflict with the rest of the world on the part of this family but that they pity other people for not being capable of participating in the truth, or not sharing the one attitude toward the world that produces blessedness. In any case, the paranoid family sees reality otherwise than does the world around it. And they cling unalterably to the belief that their view of reality is the right one. The effort required to maintain their neurotic falsification of reality serves at the same time to divert great internal family tensions. The threatened disintegration of the family is prevented by directing the tension outward. The aggression is restrained through the common polarization against the outer world, from which with the help of the paranoid idea or ideology they protect themselves either by open hostility or at least by defensive isolation.

Now, frequently one may find in paranoid families one or another member still struggling against submission to the paranoid family concept. Although the family exercises the usual pressure, he refuses, for example, to endanger his association with friends or groups outside the family by committing himself to its "private illusion." He does not want to share the isolation of the rest of the family even if they subject him to reprisals and persecute him as a traitor. It can happen that such a person, because of his inner dilemma and the tension with the other family members, becomes ill and goes to see a psychotherapist. If at all possible, this endangered individual should be advised to take individual therapy to protect himself from the paranoid isolation that threatens him through submission to his family. Occasionally, children are involved—or even adults —who unmistakably are too weak to sustain the pressure of the rest of the paranoid family even with psychotherapeutic help. An attempted cure against the family would only result, with every attempt at increased self-confidence, in the individual provoking stronger reprisals from those closest to him, and thereby the patient's confidence would be gradually shattered.

For this reason, one may, after all, decide to try family therapy, so as not to give up the patient entirely, and at the same time hoping to help the whole family out of its paranoid isolation.

In such a situation, one must recognize that the defense mechanisms of a paranoid family are often just as rigid and correspondingly resistant to therapy as those of a paranoid individual. Of course, it is often quite possible to establish contact with such a family, but only at the price of giving the impression of identifying oneself at least partially with the family's abnormal concept of reality. As a therapist, one should resolve to make use of this pretense only temporarily, in order to create an indispensable relationship of trust. Once a firm transference connection has been established, one can begin to try to free the family step by step from its morbid ideas instead of mistakenly identifying oneself further with the paranoid system.

However, the therapist should not overestimate his powers. Paranoid families in the defense of their paranoid position frequently have at their disposal enormous energy. And as soon as they notice that one is trying to beguile them and that the originally offered sympathy with the paranoid concept is not genuine, they shut themselves off, and all the otherwise effective weapons of psychoanalytical technique prove useless against this armor.

This was the way, for example, the later efforts on behalf of a cardiac-neurotic boy and his mother failed, in the case of Jakob described in the monograph *Parents, Child and Neurosis*, which, to be sure, was presented principally in its pathogenic aspect:

Jakob was an illegitimate child. After his birth, his unmarried mother became a convert to a religious sect and expiated her oppressive feelings of guilt through the ascetic way of life of that sect. At the same time, she compensated for her feelings of worthlessness through the belief that as a chosen one she belonged to God's closest elite. And in addition she protected herself against instinctual temptations by means of the sect's ideology condemning the sex instinct. And then the boy, whom she had struggled with all her might to educate as a fellow warrior for the sect, began to grow up. Naturally, it meant a dangerous threat to her neurotic defense when, instead of following her teachings, he inclined to the views and life style of friends his own age and could not see why he was not allowed rough-and-tumble games and had to avoid all youthful sports. However, she was able more and more to break down his resistance. He was an especially delicate youth lacking in strength and skill at games; because he was inferior to his contemporaries and showed poor performance in school, he suffered additional humiliations. And so with her conversion tactics she could press forward toward this goal: as an obedient member of the sect he would belong to the Chosen Ones and would look with pity on the "unbelieving" other youngsters, and by proselytizing would help them to abandon their false way of life. The youth was caught in a tormenting dilemma which grew constantly more painful. After an argument with his mother, he fell ill of a cardiac neurosis, marked by pains in the heart and dread of death.

The psychotherapist brought in by the physician reported the neurotic-cardiac symptoms were the result of an unsuccessful attempt on the part of the young man to break out of the net of the paranoid system in which his mother had entangled him. Having opposed his mother, he now believed that the pains in his heart were the punishment of God she had so often prophesied for his wicked obstinacy.

The neurotic symptoms soon subsided because the young man gave up his resistance to his mother. His fear of further divine punishments had broken his will. The therapist drew the mother into intensive therapeutic work, though he failed to prevent the son from becoming more and more deeply involved in her morbid system of thought and—aside from the meetings of the sect—losing all his earlier friends. The therapist bought the propaganda writings to the sect and listened attentively to the mother's attempts to convert him, in which presently the young man took a timid part. Without this compromise on the therapist's part, the mother would have withdrawn herself and Jakob from treatment at once. She was, admittedly, building her son up to be her "little Jesus" and had no intention of releasing him from the role of her ideal self. Despite the therapist's attempts to prevent it, Jakob failed in a number of efforts at training and at work. As soon as he got into difficulties on a job, he quit, wandered about in the streets—and then took refuge with his mother, who in any case thought only about his future as a preacher for the sect and disparaged all other social obligations. Thus the therapist's efforts shattered on the invincibility of the paranoid family system, which was already too far developed by the time the treatment started.

Once a family is obsessed in a paranoid manner by an over-rated idea or ideology, it may become impossible for a family therapist to persuade the family to single-minded cooperation. The paranoid ideology need not have such eccentric characteristics as in the instance just described. The ideology may even have very progressive characteristics and its content may inspire the unqualified sympathy of the therapist. The decisive point is the degree of submission with which the family subjects itself to the ideology. Grotesquely enough, there are paranoid families that battle unitedly for the idea of an anti-authoritarian society, without noticing that they have restructured themselves into an authoritarian group and become blind fanatics. If they have problems with one another, they simply seek solution in the ideology or in projective hostility toward outside enemies. Faced by a genuine analytical self-examination, they experience the same dread as sectarian families of the type of Jakob and his mother. They fear that an illumination of their personal motives might threaten the stability which, at least to a certain degree, the completed neurotic process of idealization has provided.

17

Psychoanalysis and Family Therapy
ARE THEY LEGITIMATELY RELATED?

Psychoanalysis is the term for the psychological theory set forth by Freud's genius and developed by his followers. The theory traces a person's psychosexual development from childhood to maturity. It further traces in novel fashion the formation of the personality with special reference to unconscious elements and instinctual processes. Bound up with this is a doctrine of the dynamics of conflict in the psyche and in particular of psychologically conditioned illnesses.

Psychoanalysis, however, is also the term for a therapeutic method. It is the standard method of uncovering conflicts through psychological treatment. This method consists in part of a specific classical procedure: the doctor analyzes the inner conflicts of an analysand in four to five sessions a week over a period of several years. The analyst's standard instrument in this is interpretation. With the aid of interpretation the analyst tries to help the analysand to become acquainted with the repressed elements of his personality and consciously to come to terms with them.

As is apparent from our discussion, family therapy is necessarily somewhat different from standard psychoanalysis. The basic difference is that it does not concentrate primarily on analyzing the psychic conflicts of an individual but on uncovering the conflicts between individuals. The inner conflicts of individual family members are, of course, very seriously taken into account in analytical family therapy—not primarily for themselves but for what they mean in critical situations within the family.

Nevertheless, it would be justified to term a particular form of family therapy psychoanalytic inasmuch as it fulfills two conditions:

1. It is based on psychoanalytical theory. At the same time, it places particular emphasis on absorbing the more recent theory of the dynamics of intra-individual relationships into the system of psychoanalytical theory that was designed originally for the individual only. This is the sense in which the theoretically developed model concepts in chapters 3 to 8 are to be understood.

2. To deserve to be called psychoanalytical, family therapy must attempt to increase the insight of those taking part in the therapy into their unconscious motives for conflict and encourage them to deal with these motives. In this respect, it follows the standard method of psychoanalysis and its central principle of therapeutic intent.

Adherence to this therapeutic principle and the unequivocal orientation to psychoanalytical theory give this form of family treatment its specifically psychoanalytical character. Of course, it undergoes some modification in that it extends the treatment to the field of social conflicts and enlarges the two-person, doctor-patient arrangement. In psychoanalytical circles, these modifications were taken very seriously until a short time ago, and the chasm between the standard method and all family-therapy approaches was sharply emphasized. But attitudes seem to be changing. One evidence of this change is that recently psychoanalysts, even within the standard procedure, in certain circumstances cooperate simultaneously with the patient's relations. As late as the early fifties, in an extensive questionnaire circulated by Glover[40] among psychoanalysts in England, all answered that they acceded "most unwillingly" to a patient's wish that they should have an interview with a member of the family. This was tantamount to declaring themselves opposed to simultaneous analytical treatment of several members of the same family. Since then in the professional literature voices have increasingly been raised in favor of relaxing the prohibition in principle, on the part of the standard-method psychoanalyst, of any contact with the relatives of the patient. Extensive interviews and also at times simultaneous psychotherapeutic treatment of the marriage partner of a patient in standard analysis have been reported and defended. Thomä[90] rightly points out, for example, that one could interpret the "historical repugnance" of psychoanalysts toward contact with the relatives of their patients as an irrational "superindividual professional countertransference." And he raises the provocative question of whether analysts with this kind of emotional attitude might not intensify the conflicts in the families of their patients. The analysand might detect the negative feelings of the analyst, communicate them to his relatives, and thereby add substantially to the family vexations.

The joint treatment of the husband, wife, or parents of a patient in a standard analysis is symptomatic of the process of mutual approach of psychoanalysis and family therapy. Here intermediate forms arise, and sometimes it is difficult to know whether to speak of extended standard psychoanalysis or of family therapy.

It cannot be considered family therapy, however, if a relative is brought in only for episodic, complementary therapy so that he shall no longer through his problems disturb the analysis of the principal patient. In such a case, the therapist considers the relative only an unimportant partner who from time to time is drawn into the treatment really so that later he can be excluded the more completely. By way of comparison, one might think of two grownups discussing a problem who for a short time let a child who has been constantly, jealously interrupting take part in their conversation only to pacify him for the moment, and immediately thereafter send him out of the room. From this extension of individual analysis no family therapy can emerge, since the therapist's formulation of the group problem is subordinated to the individual problem of a member of the family.

The hesitation on the part of psychoanalysts to take to family therapy is often connected primarily with the question to what extent a "purely analytical situation" can be established in family therapy. In psychoanalytical individual therapy, as is well known, there are a series of graduated methods, from the classical "orthodox" standard method to the analytical brief therapy (treatment of a limited focus of conflict in the space of a few sessions). Psychoanalytical family therapy also has a comparable series of steps in its technical variations. In favorable circumstances, the family therapist can penetrate as deeply into the structure of a family conflict and can set in motion processes of cure that are not much more superficial than in the course of effective individual standard treatment. At the same time, he can seldom apply analytical procedures as precisely and subtly as in individual analysis. In the majority of cases, the technical procedure is "cruder." Diagnostically, of course, he must see the micropsychological structures of those taking part in the treatment. But he must not lose himself in contemplating this, because his principal duty is to come to grips with the group process as a whole. For each individual family, he has to sort out and coordinate the technical means to be used, such as interpretation, confrontation, confirmation, and other supportive measures. In this he cannot, least of all in family therapy, be guided simply by the degree of sophistication of his patients and the structure of their conflict. More than in individual therapy, he must take into consideration how much he himself can bear. As a rule, in family-therapy arrangements he must confront his patients more directly as a real person, exactly as in group therapy. He cannot maintain as distant and neutral a role as in the classical individual method. And so he may have to endure special trials because of the many-sided transference and counter-transference problems. Such problems may sometimes prevent the therapist from achieving specific profound processes and thus allow tensions to increase to a point beyond his own emotional range of tolerance. Thus, measured against the standard method, family therapy is invariably an "untidy" procedure.

Moreover, family therapy does not keep to the analytical process of rigidly subordinating the problems of the patients to a method. If the patients' conflicts cannot be made to fit certain ideal methodological measures, then one must be flexible enough to turn things around and adapt the method to the needs of the patient. When psychoanalysts discuss among themselves the modern changes in treatment, and whether the related techniques can possibly be called "psychoanalytical," outside observers may occasionally be amazed at the scrupulously moralistic tone of these debates. As though psychoanalysts, who, after all, have everywhere striven for the removal of the taboos in our social life, had a strange dread of offending against an irrational-appearing idea of purity. As though they must constantly be apprehensive about their identity and must justify themselves in the eyes of their colleagues if they attempt to treat psychic disturbances by anything but the classical, psychoanalytical individual method. This apprehension has several causes and is not entirely unreasonable. Just one factor will be briefly touched on here.

It requires an immense amount of self-control, almost impossible for the layman to imagine, for a psychoanalyst constantly to absorb and interpret his patients' psychic problems, instinctual desires, fears, and depressions and to interpret them openly instead of protecting himself from this pressure through manipulative, therapeutic methods, advice, orders, or sympathetic action. Every analyst must be constantly on the alert to retain both his open and his controlled psychoanalytical attitude toward his patients. Especially careful observance of the technical arrangements has among other purposes that of protecting the analyst from becoming overly strained. The use of the couch in the standard method, for example, was originally thought up by Freud not simply for the greater relaxation of the patient. Freud placed the analyst on a chair behind the patient for the explicit reason that the therapist would not be constantly exposed to the gaze of his analysand.[29]

Every variation of treatment that puts the analyst in a more defenseless and threatened position necessarily arouses the fear that the difficult and vulnerable structure of the psychoanalytical doctor-patient relationship might suffer serious harm. It might no longer be possible to maintain the combination, so necessary for analytical work, of highly sensitive receptivity (the most subtle intellectual labor) and precisely timed, cautiously explanatory interventions. Therefore, it is a perfectly legitimate tendency of psychoanalysts to wish to protect as much as they can their young colleagues eager for discovery from becoming involved in risky therapeutic novelties and possibly losing their standing as psychoanalysts. Anyone in the field of psychoanalysis who overreaches himself in too difficult a treatment arrangement can in fact easily fall into permanent resignation; he may finally seek refuge in manipulative treatment techniques of pure concealment, out of a chronic dread of the chaos and confusion of unmastered analytical transference and countertransference conflicts.

In spite of all doubts and hesitations, analytical group therapy and particularly analytical family therapy have now passed their period of probation. Of course, there are all kinds of charlatans trying their hand in this field, but serious analysts in increasing numbers, and even some psychoanalytical societies, have gradually declared themselves in favor of systematically developing these new methods and scientifically extending them as fruitful new social applications of psychoanalysis. Many who were originally skeptical have by now convinced themselves that a doctor can maintain a clear analytical attitude in procedures of this sort and at the same time treat communications conflicts which become accessible only through these new methods.

In any case, it will not be long before the legitimate derivation of analytical family therapy from Freud's psychoanalysis is generally admitted and there is no longer doubt that it is one of the most important opportunities to extend the therapeutic usefulness of psychoanalytical knowledge in the future.

The relationship of psychoanalysis to family therapy has always had two aspects. First, there prevailed suspicious skepticism about this rapidly growing branch, and one could not say whether it would become strong and healthy or have to be lopped off the tree, whether it threatened psychoanalysis or would strengthen it. Now, to the degree that family therapy is permeated by the wealth of psychoanalytical thought and—at least to a large extent—tries to base itself on Freud's theory as its chief theoretical support, the distrust of official psychoanalysis is beginning to disappear.

In other quarters, the relationship of psychoanalysis to family therapy has never been, from the beginning, a defensive one but quite the reverse; there has been a marked feeling of friendly alliance between them. From year to year, society demands more of psychoanalysis to help solve the many problems in medicine, social service, pedagogy, penology, and so forth. From its comparatively recent struggle for social recognition, psycho-analysis has suddenly found itself exposed to such multifarious needs that it is now hardly in a position to meet even a part of the social tasks thrust upon it. Even in the fields of medicine and educational counseling, the disproportion between those seeking treatment and the supply of psychoanalytical therapeutic experts is disquieting—a result of the years of opposition on the part of universities and of the state to training psychoanalysts. This is why psychoanalysis must exert itself all the more to serve the purposes of group therapy, especially its social aspects. The standard method, with its expenditure, for one patient, of several hundred hours over three to five years, absorbs so much therapeutic capacity for so limited a number of the ill that it seems only sensible to give the social-psychological variants of psychoanalytical therapy as much leeway as possible for treat-ing suitable individuals and groups. It is fortunate that these com-paratively economical forms of therapy are available, not as substitutes of inferior quality but as genuine alternatives with, in part, specific symptoms and therapeutic goals.

It is not yet clear, of course, whether the central core of psychoanalytical family therapists will be able to keep the development of this fruitful new method of treatment within strict scientific limits. There are groups and special interests that see in family therapy and counseling an opportunity for ideologi-cal indoctrination of one kind of another. Missionary fanatics already wish family and group therapy to aim not at the uncover-ing of conflicts and a release from repression but at a harmoni-ous education denying all conflict. Their goals extend from a harmless and insipid "Be nice to one another!" to the strict adherence to standards dictated by rigid moral and theological concepts.

At all events, psychoanalysts must protect themselves from false friends and benefactors who would like to see the modern procedures of family and group therapy perverted to their special ends, and conflicts replaced by the creation of new dependencies —instead of by an extension of freedom.

BIBLIOGRAPHY

1 Ackerman, N. W.: *The Psychodynamics of Family Life*. New York, 1958.
2 ───── and M. L. Behrens: "The Family Approach and Levels of Intervention," *American Journal of Psychotherapy* 22 (1968), p. 5.
3 Adorno, Th. W.: "Postscriptum zu A. Mitscherlich: Das soziale und persönliche Ich," *Kölner Zeitschrift für Soziologie und Sozialpsychologie* 18 (1966), p. 37.
4 Balint, M.: *Thrills and Regression*. New York, London, 1959.
5 Beckmann, D., H. E. Richter, and J. Scheer: "Kontrolle von Psychotherapieresultaten" *Psyche* 23 (1969), p. 805.
6 ───── and H. E. Richter: *Giessen-Test, ein Test für Individual- und-Gruppendiagnostik*. Bern, Stuttgart, Vienna, 1972.
7 Bell, N. W., and E. F. Vogel: *A Modern Introduction to the Family*. London, 1960.
8 Bibring, G. L.: "Old Age: Its Liabilities and Its Assets," R. M. Loewenstein et al., ed.: in *Psychoanalysis—a General Psychology* (Essays in Honor of H. Hartmann). New York, 1966.
9 Bornstein, S.: "Unbewusstes der Eltern in der Erziehung der Kinder," *Zeitschrift für psychoanalytische Pädagogik* 8 (1934), p. 353.
10 Boszormenyi-Nagy, J., and J. L. Framo: *Intensive Family Therapy*. New York, 1965.

11 Brill, N. Q., and H. A. Storrow: "Social Class and Psychiatric Treatment," *Archives of General Psychiatry* 3 (1960), p. 340.

12 Brody, S.: "Simultaneous Psychotherapy of Married Couples," in J. Massermann, ed.: *Current Psychiatric Therapies*. New York, 1961.

13 Burlingham, D. T.: "Child Analysis and the Mother," *Psychoanalytic Quarterly* 4 (1935), p. 69.

14 ———, A. Goldberger, and A. Lussier: "Simultaneous Analysis of Mother and Child," *Psychoanalytic Study of the Child* 10 (1955), p. 165.

15 Chance, E.: *Families in Treatment*. New York, 2nd ed., 1960.

16 Christian, P., B. Hase, and W. Kromer: "Statistische Untersuchungen über die sogenannten 'Nervösen Herz- und Kreislaufs örungen,'" *Archiv für Kreislaufforschung* 20 (1954), p. 287.

17 Cleckley, H.: *The Mask of Sanity*, St. Louis, Mo., 4th ed., 1964.

18 ———: "Psychopathic States," in *American Handbook of Psychiatry*, Vol. 1. New York, 1959.

19 Dicks, H. V.: "Experiences with Marital Tensions in the Psychological Clinic," *British Journal of Medical Psychology* 26 (1952), p. 181.

20 ———: "Object Relations Theory and Marital Studies," *British Journal of Medical Psychology* 36 (1963), p. 125.

21 Dupont, R. L., and H. Grunebaum: "Willing Victims: The Husbands of Paranoid Women," *American Journal of Psychiatry* 125 (1968), p. 151.

22 Ehrenwald, J.: *Neurosis in the Family and Patterns of Psychosocial Defense*. New York, 1963.

23 Eisenstein, V., ed.: *Neurotic Interaction in Marriage*. New York, 1956.

24 Erikson, E. H.: *Childhood and Society*. New York, London, 1950.

25 Ernst, K.: *Die Prognose der Neurosen*. Berlin, Göttingen, Heidelberg, 1959.

26 Fleck, S.: "Some General and Specific Indications for Family Therapy," *Confinia psychiatrica* 8 (1965), p. 27.

27 Freud, A.: *The Ego and the Mechanisms of Defense*. London, 1937.

28 Freud, S.: *Recommendations for Physicians on the Psycho-Analytic Method of Treatment*.

29 ———: *Further Recommendations in the Technique of Psycho-Analysis: On Beginning the Treatment*.

30 ———: *On Narcissism: An Introduction.*
31 ———: *A General Introduction to Psychoanalysis.*
32 ———: *Turnings in the Ways of Psycho-Analytic Therapy.*
33 ———: *Group Psychology and the Analysis of the Ego.*
34 ———: *The Passing of the Oedipus-Complex.*
35 ———: *Beyond the Pleasure Principle.*
36 ———: *New Introductory Lectures on Psycho-Analysis.*
37 Fürstenau, P.: "Psychoanalytische Aspekte der Frauen-Emanzipation," *Das Argument* 23 (1962), p. 15.
38 ———: *Soziologie der Kindheit.* Heidelberg, 1967.
39 Giltay, H.: "Zur Psychologie des Ichideals," *Psychoanalytische Bewegung* 3 (1932), p. 25.
40 Glover, E.: *The Technique of Psycho-Analysis.* London, 1955.
41 Greenacre, Ph.: "The Role of Transference: Practical Considerations in Relation to Psychoanalytic Therapy," *Journal of the American Psychoanalytic Association* 2 (1954), p. 671.
42 ———: "Problems of Overidealization of the Analyst and of Analysis: Their Manifestations in the Transference and Countertransference Relationship," *Psychoanalytic Study of the Child* 21 (1966), p. 193.
43 Greene, B. L., ed.: *The Psychotherapies of Marital Disharmony.* London, 1965.
44 Grotjahn, M.: *Psychoanalysis and the Family Neurosis.* New York, 1960.
45 Haley, J.: *Strategies of Psychotherapy.* New York, 1963.
46 ——— and L. Hoffmann: *Techniques of Family Therapy.* New York, London, 1967.
47 Heigl-Evers, A., and F. Heigl: *Geben und Nehmen in der Ehe.* Stuttgart, 2nd ed., 1961.
48 Heimann, M.: "The Problem of Family Diagnosis," in Eisenstein, ed.: *Neurotic Interaction in Marriage.* New York, 1956.
49 Hellmann, I., O. Friedmann, and E. Shepheard: "Simultaneous Analysis of Mother and Child," *Psychoanalytic Study of the Child* 15 (1960), p. 359.
50 Hereford, C. F.: *Changing Parental Attitudes through Group Discussion.* Texas, 1963.
51 Hollingshead, A. B., and F. Redlich: *Social Class and Mental Illness.* New York, 1958.
52 Jackson, D. D., ed.: *The Etiology of Schizophrenia.* New York, 1960.
53 ——— and J. H. Weakland: "Conjoint Family Therapy," *Psychiatry* 24 (1961), p. 30.

54 Johnson, A. M., and S. A. Szurek: "The Genesis of Antisocial Acting Out in Children and Adults," *Psychoanalytic Quarterly* 21 (1952), p. 323.

55 Johnson, G.: "Family Treatment in Psychiatric Hospitals," *Psychotherapy and Psychosomatics* 16 (1968), p. 333.

56 Jorswieck, E., and J. Katwan: "Neurotische Symptome. Eine Statistik über Art und Auftreten in den Jahren 1947, 1956 und 1965," *Zeitschrift für Psychosomatische Medezin* 13 (1967), p. 12.

57 Lampl de Groot, J.: "Ich-Ideal und Über-Ich," *Psyche* 17 (1963), p. 321.

58 Levy, D. M.: *Maternal Overprotection*. New York, 1943.

59 Levy, K.: "Simultaneous Analysis of a Mother and Her Adolescent Daughter," *Psychoanalytic Study of the Child* 15 (1960), p. 378.

60 Lidz, Th., S. Fleck, A. Cornelison, and D. Terry: "The Intrafamilial Environment of the Schizophrenic Patient," *American Journal of Orthopsychiatry* 28 (1958), p. 764.

61 ———: *The Family and Human Adaption*. New York, 1963.

62 ———, S. Fleck, and A. R. Cornelison: *Schizophrenia and the Family*. New York, 1965.

63 ———: "Familie, Sprache und Schizophrenie," *Psyche* 22 (1968), p. 701.

64 Mittelmann, B.: "Complementary Neurotic Reactions in Intimate Relationship," *Psychoanalytic Quarterly* 13 (1944), p. 479.

65 Oberndorf, C. P.: "Folie à deux," New York Neurological Society, 1933; *International Journal of Psycho-Analysis* 15 (1934), p. 14.

66 ———: "Psychoanalysis of Married Couples," *Psychoanalytic Review* 25 (1938), p. 453.

67 Offer, D., and M. Sabshin: *Normality*. New York, London, 1966.

68 Pollock, G. H.: "On Symbiosis and Symbiotic Neurosis," *International Journal of Psycho-Analysis* 45 (1964), p. 1.

69 Preuss, H. G.: *Analytische Gruppenpsychotherapie: Grundlagen und Praxis*. Munich, Berlin, Vienna, 1966.

70 ———: "Die kranke Ehe," *Aspekte der Psychoanalyse* (1969), p. 103.

71 Rangell, L.: "The Intrapsychic Process and Its Analysis—a Recent Line of Thought and Its Current Implications, *International Journal of Psychoanalysis* 50 (1969), p. 65.

72 Richter, H. E.: "Die narzisstischen Projektionen der Eltern auf das Kind," *Jahrbuch der Psychoanalyse* 1 (1960), p. 62.
73 ——: *Eltern, Kind und Neurose.* Stuttgart, 2nd ed., 1967; Reinbek, 1969.
74 ——: "Zur Theorie und Therapie von Familienneurosen aus psychoanalytischer Sicht," *Der Nervenarzt* 37 (1966), p. 1.
75 ——: "Die Familie in der Psychologischen Medizin," *Praxis der Psychotherapie* 12 (1967), p. 124.
76 ——: "Einige sozialpsychologische Aspekte der Psychologischen Medizin," *Zeitschrift für Psychotherapie* 17 (1967), p. 41.
77 ——: "Familientherapie," *Psychotherapy and Psychosomatics* 16 (1968), p. 303.
78 ——: "Probleme der Familientherapie," *Jahrbuch der Psychoanalyse* 5 (1968), p. 107.
79 —— and D. Beckmann: *Herzneurose.* Stuttgart, 1969.
80 Rodgers, T. C.: "A Specific Parameter: Concurrent Psychotherapy of the Spouse of an Analysand by the Same Analyst," *International Journal of Psycho-Analysis* 46 (1965), p. 237.
81 Ryle, A.: *Neurosis in the Ordinary Family.* London, 1967.
82 Sager, C. J.: "The Development of Marriage Therapy," *American Journal of Orthopsychiatry* 36 (1966), p. 458.
83 ——, Y. I. Masters, R. E. Ronall, and W. C. Normand: "Selection and Engagement of Patients in Family Therapy," *American Journal of Orthopsychiatry* 38 (1968), p. 715.
84 Satir, V.: *Conjoint Family Therapy.* Palo Alto, Calif., 1954.
85 Shields, J.: *Monozygotic Twins.* London, 1962.
86 Singer, M. T., and L. C. Wynne: "Thought Disorder and Family Relations of Schizophrenics," *Archives of General Psychiatry* 12 (1965), p. 187.
87 Strecker, E. A.: *Their Mothers' Sons.* Philadelphia, New York, 3rd ed., 1951.
88 Tharp, R. G.: "Marriage Roles, Child Development and Family Treatment," *American Journal of Orthopsychiatry* 35 (1965), p. 531.
89 —— and G. D. Otis: "Toward a Theory for Therapeutic Intervention in Families," *Journal of Consulting Psychology* 30 (1966), p. 426.
90 Thomä, H., and B. Thomä: "Die Rolle der Angehörigen in der psychoanalytischen Technik," *Psyche* 22 (1968), p. 802.
91 Wallace, A. F., and R. D. Fogelson: "The Identity Struggle,"

in Boszormenyi-Nagy and Framo, ed.: *Intensive Family Therapy.* New York, 1965.

92 Watson, A. S.: "The Conjoint Psychotherapy of Marriage Partners," *American Journal of Orthopsychiatry* 33 (1963), p. 912.

93 Weakland, J. H.: "The 'Double-Bind' Hypothesis of Schizophrenia and Three-Party Interaction," in Jackson, ed.: *The Etiology of Schizophrenia.* New York, 1960.

94 Williams, F. S.: "Family Therapy: A Critical Assessment," *American Journal of Orthopsychiatry* 37 (1967), p. 912.

95 Wynne, L. C.: "Some Indications and Contraindications for Exploratory Family Therapy," in Boszormenyi-Nagy and Framo, ed.: *Intensive Family Therapy.* New York, 1965.

INDEX

ABOUT THE AUTHOR

Terry Gibbs started her political life as an activist and popular educator working in solidarity with various social movements in Latin America. She has since lived, worked and conducted research around the world, landing in such places as a Palestinian refugee camp in Lebanon, a Marxist guerrilla camp in Colombia, a biodiversity farm in India and a Buddhist monastery in Thailand. She also enjoys hanging out with her family, gardening and cooking. Terry currently teaches international politics at Cape Breton University in Nova Scotia, Canada, and is co-author, with Garry Leech, of *The Failure of Global Capitalism: From Cape Breton to Colombia and Beyond* (2009).